KNOW THE PAST, FIND THE FUTURE

The New York Public Library at 100

KNOW THE PAST, FIND THE FUTURE

The New York Public Library at 100

Produced and edited by

CARO LLEWELLYN

Photography by

BEOWULF SHEEHAN

FOREWORD

The year 2011 marks the centennial of The New York Public Library and the 65th anniversary of Penguin Classics. These two institutions—one of the world's preeminent libraries and the leading publisher of classics in the English-speaking world—share much in regard to their respective aims and values: the spread of literacy, the preservation of our global cultural heritage, the fostering of a love of books and literature, the importance of open access to the arts, and the broadening of our horizons. In light of these simultaneous anniversaries, our two organizations decided to create and publish—together, as a joint project—the book you are now holding. We hope you read it and enjoy it, and we encourage you, in the spirit of a library book, to share it with friends, family, acquaintances, and anyone you know who loves to read.

—Kathryn Court, president and publisher of Penguin Books

PAUL LeCLERC, president and CEO of The New York Public Library, with the bronze portrait bust of Voltaire by Jean-Antoine Houdon from 1778

INTRODUCTION

Libraries are the earliest and most enduring cultural entity.

Since their origins in Mesopotamia five thousand years ago, libraries have had only three main purposes, all revolving around collections: to acquire them; to preserve them; and to make them accessible, customarily in highly restricted ways.

What sets The New York Public Library apart from all the libraries that have existed is not that it has amassed, over the past one hundred years—thanks to the taste and brilliance of its curators—one of the greatest collections in history.

Rather it is that the Library has put this magisterial collection at the disposal of literally everyone on the planet.

As opposed to all other great library collections, which are essentially closed to the public, ours is explicitly and deliberately made accessible to all.

Our founders created this radically different paradigm of access a century ago. So that their intentions would be forever present to the public, they chiseled into the marble walls of the great entrance hall two ringing, inspiring affirmations.

The first states the principle of free access: "The City of New York erected this building to be maintained forever as a free Library for the use of the People."

And the second stresses the essential connection the founders saw between access and a democratic society: "On the diffusion of education among the People rest the preservation and perpetuation of our free institutions."

Many generations have already "found the future" by exploiting the Library's massive collections to explore, discover, invent, and to create new knowledge and new works of the imagination.

How does one even begin to capture the contribution to culture and to civil society that a century's worth of readers here have made because of our collections and staff expertise?

One way is to present, as we do in this centennial volume, the reflections of one hundred of today's notable figures on what the collections mean to them.

They represent the contemporary generation of grateful readers.

I hope the eloquence and beauty of their texts will then inspire us to imagine all the wonderful tales that could be told by countless readers and writers of past generations, all in tribute to this most magnanimous, most wonderful of libraries.

I am deeply grateful to all the writers who have contributed to this precious volume, to Penguin Classics for having published it pro bono, to Caro Llewellyn, who conceived it and made it happen, and to Beowulf Sheehan for his exquisite portraits. You couldn't have given the Library a more fitting centennial birthday present.

And in the spirit of access to all, we're giving you this beautiful book free of charge and hope you will share it with others—pass it along—just as we pass along our millions of library books every day.

—Paul LeClerc, president of The New York Public Library

P.S. My favorite item in the collections at the Stephen A. Schwarzman Building is the bronze portrait bust of Voltaire by Jean-Antoine Houdon, signed and dated 1778.

KNOW THE PAST, FIND THE FUTURE

The New York Public Library at 100

LAURIE ANDERSON, performance artist, musician, and inventor

LAURIE ANDERSON

Declaration of Independence

July 4, 1776

hen I got the wish list of things I could see from the collection I was completely overwhelmed. I began to try to narrow it down by circling my favorites. Soon the paper was a mass of interlocking circles. There was almost nothing I didn't want to see.

When I was a kid I had the rather odd hobby of making my own colonial newspapers. These were reports of the doings in a small town—new laws, property sales, decrees, and gossip modeled on some imaginary New England town. I hand-copied the shaky type of mid-eighteenth-century newspapers and handed them out to my neighbors, who filed them on their back porches.

The story behind these papers was the national myth we almost unconsciously absorbed as kids—the story of rebellion, independence, and freedom, a story hundreds of years old but still dynamic and strangely inspiring even as the empire seemed to be disappearing.

So when I numbered my wish list, the Declaration of Independence was on the top. When they brought it out in its frame—complete with the somewhat shaky type and the actual paper made from rags in one of the little colonial towns—I was suddenly tearful, in awe. Our national heritage and birthright in print.

Other treasures included a print depicting the blunt topped reservoir that stood on the site where the Library now stands; a topographical cutout one-of-a-kind book by Maya Lin; a page from William Blake with the slogan "to annihilate the selfhood of deceit and false forgiveness" inscribed on a banner at the bottom of the page; some paperbacks, including *The Mademoiselle Career Girl's Guide to New York* by Faye Hammel from 1962, *Night Side of New York—A Picture of the Great Metropolis After Nightfall* by "Members of the New York Press," containing illustrations of men breaking into buildings (pictured right); and *A Guide for the Woman Vacationist* by Marjorie Hillis, author of *Live Alone and Like It.*

On the way out we stopped at an exhibition of several religions—a collection of small relics and various manuscripts.

Part of the display that caught my eye was a phrase from a timeline of Christian milestones: "ca. 1700 B.C.E. Abraham enters into a covenantal relationship with a single, unseeable God." That covered it.

09782
PRICE TWENTY-FIVE CENTS.
NIGHT SIDE
OF NEW YORK
PUBLISHED BY J. C. HANEY & Co. 109 NASSAU STREET N.Y.
The American News Company, Agents.

KWAME ANTHONY APPIAH, philosopher, cultural theorist, and novelist

KWAME ANTHONY APPIAH

OUR LIBRARY

Poems on Various Subjects, Religious and Moral, Phillis Wheatley

1773

One of my favorite paintings is in the Scuola di S. Giorgio degli Schiavoni in Venice. It's known, usually, as *St. Jerome in His Study.* The oil shows a bearded man, seated at a desk in priestly robes, his pen raised as if he has been distracted for a moment from his writing, looking raptly up through what must be a window to his left, outside the frame of the painting, the light from which casts sharp shadows throughout the space. Behind him is a small altar, with a large statue holding a crucifix, a bishop's miter and crosier resting to its left and right. Toward the front of the scene, to the left, a small dog sits watching. And along the wall, on the left of the painting, is the end of a single row of books . . . perhaps a few dozen of them.

The painting is the work of the Venetian painter Vittore Carpaccio. It was completed in the very early sixteenth century, probably in about 1502. If it were a picture of St. Jerome—who is the undoubted subject of the two paintings to his left—the scene depicted would have taken place in the later part of the fifth century, for the figure is a young man, his beard not yet turned to gray; the other pictures of St. Jerome in the Scuola show him with a white beard . . . presumably, therefore, in the early sixth century, since he died in about 420.

As it happens, though, the painting, despite its customary name, is not of St. Jerome; and the event it pictures can confidently be set in 420, since it represents—as I learned from an article by Helen Roberts in *The Art Bulletin* for December 1959—the moment of a vision that St. Augustine had on the day of Jerome's death. Not that this matters much for the value of the painting as historical evidence, since, as was normal in Carpaccio's day, the painter has represented the great father of the church clothed in the style of his own day and in a room much like that of a scholar of his own time. Which brings me back to that little shelf of books.

Carpaccio was representing the world of one great teacher, one of the greatest of the Father's of the Church, caught in a vision of another. To symbolize that for his own time he showed someone with a significant library. And a great private library, the library of a scholar, in the Renaissance would have had—by the standards of our own day—only a very few books. Michel Eyquem, Sieur de Montaigne, who wrote about his own marvelous library in the later sixteenth century—his *Essays* first appeared in 1580, half a century after Carpaccio's death—was justly proud that he owned about one and a half thousand volumes, many of them left to him by his beloved friend, the lawyer-humanist Étienne de La Boétie.

In the *Essays* Montaigne describes the circular room at the top of a tower on the windswept hill that gave his estate its name; the room to which he came on his thirty-eighth birthday, writing on the beam above his bookshelves that he had "retired to the bosom of the learned virgins, where in calm and freed from all cares he will spend what little remains of his life . . ." In the same inscription he called this room a "sweet sanctuary . . . consecrated to his freedom, tranquility, and leisure."

Montaigne's library contained a wonderfully diverse range of reading, from the super serious—his edition of Lucretius's *On the Nature of Things,* heavily annotated in his own hand, can be seen in the Cambridge University Library—to what he once called the "*simplement plaisans*" (the simply delightful), among which he included Boccaccio's *Decameron* and Rabelais among the moderns, but also, certainly, Virgil, Horace, and Catullus (along with Lucretius) among the ancients.

The shelf of less than a hundred books in Augustine's study would have had in it most of the books that Augustine thought worth reading;

Montaigne was delighted with his library and would probably have thought that it had most of what he, too, needed. After all, Montaigne was enormously rich by the standards of his day. He could look out from that tower and be pretty confident that in every direction there was no one whose house he could see who had as many books as he did; and while there were great libraries at religious institutions and at the University in Bordeaux, forty miles away, most people did not have access to them. But the richest person in the world today would have a hard time acquiring a copy of most of the books that he or she thought worth reading. You know, if you are a contemporary reader, that you have choices to make among a vast multitude of options and that you simply don't have the lifetimes it would take to read all the worthwhile books that are already in print. I struggle all the time with that thought: each book I chose is an insignificant fraction of the human library, but a significant fraction of the few thousand books I will ever read.

And here's the thing: every book in Montaigne's library (like the article I mentioned in *The Art Bulletin,* like scores of books about St Jerome, St. Augustine, and Carpaccio) is available to me in the reading rooms of The New York Public Library. That in itself is a quite amazing fact. There are few libraries in the world—the Library of Congress, the British Library, the Bibliothèque Nationale in Paris, the Widener Library at Harvard—where you can be equally confident that that is so. On a vast range of topics, the same is true: most of what you would need to read to pursue a serious study of the subject is available in The New York Public Library. And to use this library, all you have to do is show up in New York.

In fact, you don't even have to show up. The Library does an astonishing public service to more than those who visit its shelves and its reading rooms. It provides, on the Web, a catalog of its collections (and access to lots of other information) that is available to anyone anywhere. That is why I could find out, before I got there, that if I wanted to see—and I did—a copy of the 1773 first edition of Phillis Wheatley's *Poems on Various Subjects, Religious and Moral,* I could present myself at the special collections of the Schomburg Center. I could also not just see but hold in my hand a copy of a "Prayer of Phillis's accidentally discovered in her Bible. Sabbath, June 13, 1779," something written in a hand I cannot read, but with a carefully typed transcription to allow me to circumvent my own infirmity. I could look at the first editions of

Phillis's letters; read a book containing George Washington's invitation to her to visit him, if she could, after his receipt of her poem. "If you should ever come to Cambridge, or near Head Quarters, I shall be happy to see a person so favoured by the Muse . . . ," Washington wrote.

I saw a dozen books and manuscripts in an hour at the Schomburg Center that are connected with the life and work of Phillis Wheatley. I saw, too, something I didn't expect: a copy she herself had signed. To know that you are holding in your hand a copy of a book whose American author signed before the birth of the American republic, that is truly a magical thing.

The online catalog—the digital key to the treasures of The New York Public Library—is therefore itself a treasure. But, for me at least, it remains true that there is nothing like the book itself. And, as a sometime New Yorker, I can find that nourishing contact with books, which Carpaccio hinted at and Montaigne celebrated, whenever I chose; and the Library—which, when I am there, is all mine—has ten thousand times the number of books that Montaigne created for his "freedom, tranquility, and leisure." And all available not just to one rich and solitary genius, but to thousands of us every day.

REZA ASLAN, writer and scholar of religions

REZA ASLAN

Firdausī Tūsī's *Shāhnāmah* (Book of Kings),
anonymous artist
copied 1614 in Shīrāz for Muhammed Sharīf by Muhammed 'Alī,
opaque watercolor, ink and gold leaf,
illustrations added circa 1900–1925,
Spencer Collection

Written more than a thousand years ago by Abolqasem Firdausī, the *Shāhnāmah,* or Book of Kings, recounts the mythological history of Iran from the first moments of creation to the Arab conquest of the Persian Empire in the seventh century A.D. Legend says that Firdausī composed the *Shāhnāmah* under the patronage of Sultan Mahmud of Ghazna, who promised him one dinar for every couplet he wrote. But when Firdausī presented nearly 60,000 couplets, a flustered Mahmud offered him a fraction of his promised reward. Insulted, Firdausī rejected the money and returned home to the city of Tus, where he died impoverished and embittered. But his poem endured.

The *Shāhnāmah* is often compared to Homer's *Iliad* and *Odyssey,* and certainly it has much in common with those blood-soaked epics about gods and men in conflict with each other and themselves. Others find its literary equivalent in Milton's *Paradise Lost* or Dante's *Divine Comedy,* as it shares with those master works an obsession with the eternal battle between the cosmic forces of Good and Evil. But in truth, it is difficult to find another epic in any language that has had as profound an impact in shaping and preserving a people's identity.

For many Iranians, the *Shāhnāmah* links past and present, forming a cohesive mythology through which they understand their place in the world. It is the very core and essence of Persian identity. Its stories and myths pulse through the veins of every Iranian around the world. In short, the *Shāhnāmah* is not just a poem; it is Iran's national scripture. And Firdausī is no mere poet; he is Iran's national prophet.

It is for this reason that the *Shāhnāmah* has often been used as a weapon in the historical struggle between the turban and the crown in Iran. The Pahlavi Shahs, who came to power in 1925, promoted study of the poem as a means of de-emphasizing the country's Islamic heritage and thus stripping the clerics of their ideological authority. They commissioned an official edition of the *Shāhnāmah* and compelled schoolchildren to memorize passages that emphasized the glories of kingly rule. The last Shah, Mohammed Reza Pahlavi brazenly linked his rule to that of the semi-divine kings of the *Shāhnāmah*.

After the 1979 revolution and the creation of the Islamic Republic of Iran, the clerical regime began a vigorous campaign to cleanse the new country of its pre-Islamic past, including the *Shāhnāmah*. Ayatollah Ruhollah Khomeini considered the book to be an offensive, even sacrilegious, text that explicitly endorsed monarchy; he discouraged public readings of it.

Today, as a new generation of Iranians struggles to define itself in opposition to a widely reviled religious regime, the *Shāhnāmah* is re-emerging as the supreme expression of a cultural identity, transcending all notions of politics or piety. Yet the world that Firdausī conjured up a thousand years ago—a world of grotesque monsters and valiant heroes, petty kings and epic battles, love found and love lost—is one that all peoples everywhere recognize, which is why it has been such a deep influence on so many people and cultures, not just throughout Asia and the Middle East but across the world. C.S. Lewis, J.R.R. Tolkien, George Lucas, Jerry Bruckheimer—all owe a great debt to the world created by Firdausī. Indeed, the myths and stories, lessons and values of the *Shāhnāmah* are ones that remain as relevant today as they did a millennium ago.

WILLIAM F. BAKER, distinguished professor of education at the Fordham University Graduate School of Education

WILLIAM F. BAKER

REFLECTIONS FOR THE LIBRARY'S ANNIVERSARY

The Arctic Regions, William Bradford

London, 1873. Photography Collection,
The Miriam and Ira D. Wallach Division of Art,
Prints and Photographs

I read my way to the South Pole long before I ever set foot there. Books by Scott, Shackleton, and Byrd opened up spaces in my boyhood imagination as wide as the vast landscapes their authors describe. Much has since populated those spaces—my education, my career, my family, the books I have written, and decades of life experience, including two trips to the South Pole and one to the North—but there is still room for more. Wonder is infinite. And if knowledge begins in wonder, as Socrates says, I would add that for me, wonder began in books.

I imagine it was the same for the great men of polar exploration's heroic age. They certainly had a deep regard for the printed word. They carried books with them on their sea voyages, and on their backs into places where a bit of extra weight could mean the difference between life and death. Photographs of Shackleton's stranded South Pole expedition show bearded, swaddled men at rest in the cramped cabins of their ship, surrounded everywhere by the spines and covers of books. It is romantic yet practical that those early explorers took so many books with them, sometimes even the entire *Encyclopedia Britannica*. Books were their sole source of entertainment and knowledge during the years of isolation on the long trip from civilization to the poles, a trip that was too often a one-way ticket. On a slow boat to probable death, who wouldn't want a good book or two?

I know of at least one book, one of the rarest on earth, that made the one-way trip in the other direction, from the Antarctic to civilization. It is called *Aurora Australis,* which means "light of the south," and I believe it is the only book ever entirely published, from typesetting to binding, in Antarctica. Shackleton and his men actually shipped a printing press across thousands of miles of ocean, and set it up in a seven-foot by-seven-foot room already crammed with gear and the sleeping quarters of two men. What but a near religious reverence for books would make men share Antarctic quarters with a machine that gave no warmth but the certain knowledge that they would be the first in history on their new continent to publish a book? They wanted to signal the arrival of civilization. They also wanted to turn a handsome profit back home on their limited print run, which, as with most publishing ventures, never materialized. In the end, they gave most of their copies away.

Decades later I would be the first in history to bring television cameras to the South Pole. I would also barely break even on a harebrained scheme to sell individually packaged chunks of prehistoric arctic ice at fancy department stores. In the end, I gave most of the ice away. A sincere wish to carry knowledge to the earth's remote places and a dash of showmanship have ever gone hand in hand in the annals of polar exploration.

I am proud of my polar exploits. Before I stood on both poles, I dispatched researchers to The New York Public Library to see how many people had done it before. They brought back a few different numbers, and I happily chose the lowest, which was eighth in all of human history.

The actual moments I spent at each pole constitute mere hours of my life at most. I have spent far longer imagining and then remembering my adventures, finding new meanings for them, exploring new corners of that space that books so long ago opened up in my imagination.

ISHMAEL BEAH, writer

ISHMAEL BEAH

Treasure Island, Robert Louis Stevenson

early illustrated edition, 1887

esterday I held in my hands a very fragile copy of the first edition of *Treasure Island* by Robert Louis Stevenson at The New York Public Library on 42nd Street. The age of the book itself gently commanded a care that I couldn't resist. As I turned the pages, slower than I had ever turned leaflets of any book, I made sure to press my finger deeply into each page to become part of the life of the words and pictures. The odor from the pages lingered on my fingers for many hours afterward. And every now and then, I removed my hands from my jacket pocket and allowed my nose to taste the smell of a past that I can only try to comprehend. However, each smell of my hands rekindled a memory of my encounter with *Treasure Island* when I was a boy in my small town in Sierra Leone. It was my first year of secondary school and my English teacher had a copy of the book, the only copy, which he read to us, acting out every character. He even rearranged the classroom, adding a makeshift apple barrel and a mast made out of bamboo, and assigned us each a character from the novel. With handwritten lines on pieces of paper that the teacher had handed us, we acted out *Treasure Island,* and I was Jim Hawkins perhaps because I was the youngest in my class. This was one of the first books I was introduced to that had a central character and narrator, for most of the story, who was a boy. It was also the first narrative that gave permission to my imagination to depart my own landscape and experience another world. From that day on, I discovered a valuable treasure of my own: the love and power of words.

Yesterday, as I washed my hands, reluctantly, I was reminded again of the importance of imagination for every human being—and that words for me will always be my passport to travel to lands unknown, a weapon to correct misunderstandings about my humanity, and an antidote to cure all illnesses of the human condition. Even though the odor from the pages of *Treasure Island* is gone, the memory of its words and the feelings they revived within me remain forever.

SAMANTHA BEE, actress and author

SAMANTHA BEE

Young Girl, Cotton Picker, from the series *American Country Woman,* Dorothea Lange

gelatin silver print, 1941, Photography Collection, The Miriam and Ira D. Wallach Division of Art, Prints and Photograph

---

Before we go any further together, let's get this out of the way first: I am a photography neophyte. In fact, prior to moving to the city in 2003, my only experience of The New York Public Library was a scene from the movie *Ghostbusters* and a general feeling that it might be a place I would get kicked out of for slipping copies of my book into the dust jackets of Faulkner's Yoknapatawpha saga. Don't think I wouldn't do it.

So it was with no small measure of humility that I ascended the steps of the Library for private access to something exceptional: Dorothea Lange's *American Country Woman* series of photographs. As the curator stood quietly by my side guiding me through the collection, I felt him subtly analyzing my fingertips for fudge residue, and tried not to be intimidated by the incongruousness of letting someone like me, who once professionally dressed as a hamburger, touch something so historically and culturally significant.

The photographs are beautiful, of course. They are candid and powerful, and convey a sense of time and place and hardship that no words could. In the eyes of her subjects, I saw innocence and weariness, pride, fear for the future, despair. I saw deep chasms of sorrow, grinding poverty, and the grim determination in the face of a mother who can't find food for her family. In an instant I remembered what I should already know: that we come from somewhere. That we're not the first generation of people who ever lived on this earth, who ever put our hands in the dirt, who ever loved our children hard.

Now that I officially can't shake these images from my mind, and hope I never do, I will cherish the memory of this experience and the feeling of intense gratitude it left me with.

Also, I'm not going to tell you where I left them, but you're welcome in advance for the books.

STAFF OF THE HENRY W. AND ALBERT A. BERG COLLECTION OF ENGLISH AND AMERICAN LITERATURE (l to r): Rebecca Filner, librarian; Isaac Gewirtz, curator; Anne Garner, librarian

HENRY W. AND ALBERT A. BERG COLLECTION OF ENGLISH AND AMERICAN LITERATURE

Autograph Letter by Charlotte Brontë
Signed to Ellen Nussey
Haworth, Dec. [22], 1848

"The Waste Land," T.S. Eliot
typescript, 1921–22

The Westmoreland Ms. of John Donne's Poems
ca. 1620

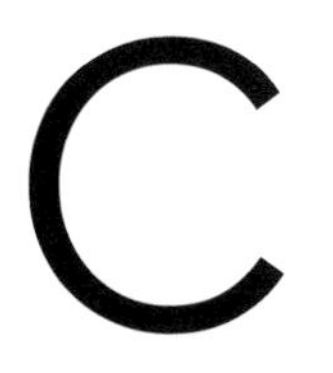

harlotte and Emily Brontë have always been two of my favorite authors, in part because their secluded and tragic lives fascinate me. Two elder Brontë sisters died in childhood, and three of the four Brontë siblings who made it to adulthood died in quick succession between September 1848 and May 1849.

In this letter, Charlotte Brontë writes to her close friend, Ellen Nussey, to ask her to come to Haworth following Emily Brontë's death from tuberculosis. Emily, Charlotte writes, "never will suffer more in this world—she is gone after a hard, short conflict . . . there is no Emily in Time or in Earth now—yesterday we put her poor, wasted mortal frame quietly under the Church pavement." Charlotte reports that the family is "very calm at present," but she also notes that she "never so much needed the consolation of a friend's presence."

For me, this letter poignantly conveys both Charlotte Brontë's anguish at losing Emily and her anxiety for the health of her father and her remaining sister, Anne. I am able to understand an inkling of what it must have been like for Charlotte to lose her siblings as I look at her neat, hurried hand filling the page. —*Rebecca Filner*

I begin by confessing that I have no "favorite" item in the Berg Collection. This might not be the case were the collection composed solely of published texts. Then, I might have chosen my favorite book by my favorite author—*Pale Fire,* by Vladimir Nabokov. But the Berg, though wondrously comprehensive in first editions, has become the destination for so many literature graduate students, scholars, and writers chiefly because almost every important English-language writer and poet from the late eighteenth to the mid-twentieth century is represented by their manuscripts or letters, journals or diaries, and often by numerous examples of all of these genres. The texts embodied in them are alive in a way that their published and better known avatars are not. This does not mean that a rough draft of a poem or novel is "better" than its published text. (Though we should remember that an unpublished draft may be every bit as polished as the published text, though different, and indeed "better," remaining unknown to most readers simply because the publisher or author chose, for any of several predictable reasons, not to publish it.) By "alive" I mean that such manuscripts and typescripts bear the marks of their creators' struggles, as well as those of their editors, thereby revealing their creators' minds and intentions in ways that cleanly printed pages cannot.

Now, by this standard, it could be argued, I should have chosen the manuscript of a book of poetry by the greatest English-language poet since Wordsworth—that is, W.B. Yeats, whose papers the Berg holds in greater number than any other institution in the world excepting the National Library of Ireland. Instead, I chose the typescript/manuscript of "The Waste Land," containing Ezra Pound's severe excisions, accompanied by his comments, occasionally derisive, and notes by Eliot's first wife, Vivien. I chose "The Waste Land" not only because it is a great poem (Yeats wrote several that are greater), but because it is a pioneering poem, one which expresses with force and subtlety not only Eliot's sensibility and concerns, but those of his peers—the artists, writers, and thinkers who could no longer bear to look at the world through the clouded lens of idealism, religious clichés, and sentiment. Wondrous, brave, terrified, they were impelled to confront the human mind as it is in its moment to moment reactions, in its shabby evasions, and in its occasional exaltations. Modernism, however else we may regard it, was a struggle to discover what it meant to be human when the authority of the past was overthrown. "The Waste Land" dramatized how a mind formed by the moral and aesthetic values of the ancient classics (and their more recent progeny) fractured under the casual brutishness of a society in which those values have lost all meaning and in which references to them have been reduced to a form of social currency exchanged by hollow people engaged in sterile conversations.

What really goes on in a desperate middle-aged man's over-educated head as he stands in a stuffy pub beneath the doom of closing hour, nursing a last drink and strained nerves, as he overhears bits of conversation about bad teeth, mechanical seductions, betrayals, and abortions? Eliot looked at it hard and found himself compelled to show it to us, to himself, really. "HURRY UP PLEASE IT'S TIME." His vision was harrowing, hilarious, learnedly allusive (endnotes, though these were omitted from the poem's first publication, in the *Criterion,* in October 1922), profound, occasionally prissy, and curiously prescient in its turn to Eastern spiritual traditions as a kind of Greek chorus's reproof to the modern West's failure of mind and heart. In the typescript, we see Eliot's original, more expansive conception of the poem, as well as his unfortunate tendency to abstraction, which Pound checked. (Eliot describing London: "Responsive to the momentary need, / Vibrates unconscious to its formal destiny," mercifully deleted by Pound.) As much as the typescript shows us Eliot's creative imagination, it shows us Pound's, and in the combination becomes a master's primer for modernist poetry. A favorite for our age, if not the ages.

—*Isaac Gewirtz*

The Westmoreland manuscript dates to ca.1620 and is the earliest and most complete source for Donne's poetry. It contains nineteen of Donne's Holy Sonnets (and is the sole source for three of these). It was copied out, presumably from Donne's own drafts by his law school buddy Rowland Woodward, and likely given to the Earl of Westmoreland as a gift (the item remained with his descendants for almost 250 years). The Westmoreland is the oldest manuscript in the Berg Collection, and a great example of original source material that greatly enhances our understanding of important texts.

The poet of the Holy Sonnets was a poet in crisis. Donne had eloped with Anne More, niece of his patron, Lord Ellesmere, a move that left him broke, imprisoned, and for a time, without a patron. "John Donne, Anne Donne, Un-donne," he allegedly dead-panned. He had ten young children to support, and was torn about whether to abandon Catholicism and convert to Anglicanism. The Holy Sonnets trenchantly explore that conflict.

Donne's poetry feels modern in its emphasis on the psychological. His voice in both his seduction and religious poetry is electrifying—and immediate. I love how artfully Donne embraces the chaos in his mind to craft poems that stand as permanent as cathedrals. Searching and contradictory, they are near perfect artifacts of Donne's own inner struggles to reconcile the divergent spiritualities within him.

—*Anne Garner*

MICHAEL R. BLOOMBERG, mayor of New York City

MAYOR BLOOMBERG

Johnny Tremain, Esther Forbes

1943

Growing up, I must have read *Johnny Tremain* a hundred times. Esther Forbes's children's novel is about a daring teenage messenger who tells Paul Revere what to watch for in the church tower on the night of his famous ride: "One, if by land, and two, if by sea . . . " I grew up in Medford, Massachusetts, only a short train ride from Boston and the Revolutionary War sites described in the book. The history came alive for me when reading it, just like when I visited all those historic places. And the book connects to one of my proudest childhood memories. One year I was picked from my Boy Scout troop to recite the famous Longfellow poem "Paul Revere's Ride" for the crowd assembled for Patriots' Day in Medford Square, which was a major holiday in Massachusetts. Up onstage, the high school band playing the music of John Philip Sousa, "Paul Revere" galloping by on his horse, newspaper photographers snapping away, all the pageantry and patriotism made me feel connected to the great history of our nation. It's a day I will never forget—and I know it was a day I made my parents proud. The values my parents instilled in me gave me a strong sense of responsibility to others, and that's what led me to philanthropy and, ultimately, to run for mayor. Still today, I do the best I can to serve others, stand up for what is right, and make a difference in the world—just like Johnny Tremain.

ROY BLOUNT, JR., actor, author, playwright, and screenwriter

(previous pages)

ROY BLOUNT, JR., meets Pooh

ROY BLOUNT, JR.

I MEET POOH

The Real Winnie-the-Pooh

A.A. Milne's gift to his son, Christopher Robin, on his first birthday, August 1, 1921

Once in the California Angels' press box in the early '70s, I stood, turned from the game, and found myself eyeball to eyeball with Jack Benny.

My parents and I, together, when I was a little child, loved Jack Benny. Listened to him, on the radio, as regularly as we went to church. I can still hear the voices of Jack and all his friends—Rochester, Mary Livingstone, Phil Harris, Mr. Kitzel . . .

And there he was, in Anaheim, inches away. My childhood came bursting back, and I was not ready to field it. "Hurrah!" I should have shouted. "Your radio show, sir, was one of my earliest prime delights." No, not that, but something heartfelt, something appropriate to the moment. Maybe just, "Hoo-*hooo,* Meester Beenie," in the voice of Mr. Kitzel.

I was struck dumb. Not just speechless, but stupid. I could feel my eyes bugging and my lips moving up and down. Benny looked alarmed, even threatened, and scooted past me, out of the press box, into the depths of my past.

I didn't want it to be like that with Winnie-the-Pooh. (Don't forget the hyphens, as in *Moby-Dick.*) Going in, I knew that I would be seeing the stuffed bear on whom A.A. Milne based the Pooh character, because I had selected him from a wide range of treasures held by The New York Public Library. Still I think *frisson* would not be too strong a word for what I felt on seeing the old boy in the, so to speak, flesh.

I couldn't touch him because he was fragile, but he looked pretty good. Patched here and there, but in better shape than his friends, who were still in a glass case: Eeyore, Tigger, Piglet, Kanga, and Roo . . . Eeyore, of course, looked droopy, because that was his character. Eeyore had gravitas, because Eeyore was sad.

My mother read to me, and taught me to read, from other books as well. I'd have to say B'rer Rabbit was a bigger influence. But the Pooh books, at least on the surface, were more intimate and soothing. In some ways they were like later generations' Little Bear stories and *Goodnight Moon,* which I associate with my kids rather than my mother.

The author's son, Christopher Milne, on whom his father based the Christopher Robin character, played as a child with these very stuffed animals. In adulthood Christopher wrote a disgruntled memoir about the downside of being Christopher Robin. Dorothy Parker, in her role as *Esquire* magazine's Constant Reader, wrote of *The House at Pooh Corner,* "Tonstant Weader thwowed up."

Well, I wrote a disgruntled memoir myself. Who hasn't? And Dorothy Parker wasn't exactly Sophocles herself.

And what did you want my mother to read to me when I was a toddler, *Les Misérables*? She was at some level miserable herself—at any rate, I can remember her evincing an identification with Eeyore. She wanted reading to be a happy time.

I wouldn't dig up my childhood copies of the Pooh books, they're still too raw. But when I got an iPad, an iBook of *Winnie-the-Pooh* was already loaded onto it. And okay, *Winnie-the-Pooh* starts out twee—Milne Senior talking to Christopher and the reader at the same time, "Well, you laughed to yourself, 'Silly old Bear!' but you didn't say it aloud because you were so fond of him . . ."

But as the animals take over, the book gets sharper. The character Rabbit is droll. "Hallo, Rabbit," says Pooh at one point, "is that you?"

"Let's pretend it isn't," says Rabbit, "and see what happens."

"I've got a message for you," says Pooh.

"I'll give it to *him,*" says Rabbit.

Give it to him. That's pretty snappy with regard to who's who.

After I started reading to myself, I moved on to the great comic strip *Pogo*. I found many of the Pooh characters loosely recapitulated in *Pogo*.

Pooh (or Christopher): Pogo.

Eeyore: Porky Pine.

Tigger: Albert the Alligator.

Owl: Howland Owl.

Kanga and Roo: Miz Beaver and Grundoon (though the latter two are not related by blood). Actually Pup Dog is closer to Roo.

Piglet: I don't know, Churchy?

The cast of the Pooh stories is nowhere near as rich as that of *Pogo*, which include a suitably savage caricature of Senator Joseph McCarthy and a hearty phys-ed instructor chicken called Sis Boombah. Pooh doesn't know anyone sexy, certainly no one like Miss Mam'selle Hepzibah, a sweet, flirty skunk with a heavy French accent.

Pooh and friends are pre-pubescent. But he himself, the physically existent ur-Pooh, is no sweetie-kins. His face is as straight as Buster Keaton's. So Christopher had to make an imaginative effort. Pooh in the original E.H. Shepard illustrations is a shade cuter, and I can't deny I liked him that way. But the ickiness of the most recent—the Disney—version is inexcusable. Has childhood gotten softer so that children can relate to such mawkishness, or has it gotten harder so that they need it?

Thoughts such as these went through my head as I posed—and may I say, it was an honor—for photos with Winnie-the-Pooh at NYPL. I don't flatter myself that Pooh's posing with me caused anything to go through his head. But I feel I was duly responsive after all these years. I'll never quite forgive myself for not saying, "Hoo-*hooo*, Meester Beenie," but I did say, "Hullo, Pooh."

ERIC BOGOSIAN, actor, playwright, monologist, and novelist

ERIC BOGOSIAN

Firdausī Tūsī's *Tarjumah-I Shāhnāmah* (Book of Kings translated into Turkish), anonymous artist

tempera, ink and gold leaf on cream gold-sprinkled paper, 1616–1620, Spencer Collection

My family is of Armenian-Turkish origin. My grandparents were survivors of massacres in Anatolia that occurred around World War I. I am writing a book about events from that time precisely because I want to more fully understand the events of that time. I want to know what Turkey is and was. In my research, I have come to be awed by the majesty of the Ottoman Empire. The sultans are long gone, but the palaces and art they left behind are still here. I have traveled to Turkey and visited the exquisitely tiled royal harem, I have meditated under the vast domes of the major mosques, and I have walked the avenues and byways the Ottomans traveled. I have also read dozens of volumes on Turkish history and culture.

But it wasn't until I visited The New York Public Library on Fifth Avenue that I was able to handle a genuine artifact from the sultan's treasury.

Alvaro Gonzalez-Lazo, a print specialist at the Print Collection, provided me with a massive, gilt and leather-bound Turkish translation of the epic poem the *Shāhnāmah* by the great Persian poet Firdausī Tūsī. The manuscript is entirely handmade, every cream-colored gold-flecked page covered with meticulous Turkish calligraphy, interspersed with marvelous small paintings illustrating the story.

This volume is four hundred years old! Fabricated over several years around the year 1600, it was made when the Ottoman Empire was at its peak, when the sultans threatened Europe and ruled a kingdom that extended from Hungry to India and included Egypt and North Africa . . . At the time of this book's manufacture, my Armenian ancestors lived under the reign of its owner, and Europeans could only dream of entering the palatial grounds of the sultan or ever touching anything that belonged to him.

The book is a masterpiece, every page, every single character meticulously created by calligraphers at the height of their artistic powers. It takes your breath away. To think that something like this (and this is only one item of many in the Library's collection) is here in New York and available for any citizen of our great city to hold and examine is a wonderful thing. Thank you, The New York Public Library, for this shot of adrenaline as I trek through the landscape of history!

IAN BURUMA, author, journalist, and academic

IAN BURUMA

LIN BIAO'S LITTLE RED BOOK

Mao zhu xi yu lu/[Mao Zedong zhu]

(Mao's Little Red Book) 1967

t first glance, or even a second, or third (etcetera), there is nothing remarkable about the copy of *Quotations from Chairman Mao* carefully conserved by The New York Public Library. Pocket-sized, with a simple maroon plastic cover, it looks pretty much like millions of similar "Little Red Books," as they were called in the West. I've seen flashier editions, with pictures of Mao surrounded by a halo of golden sunrays, for example.

You can tell that this edition was printed before 1971, because it still has a preface by Lin Biao, one of the great generals of the Communist revolution, and once poised to be Mao's successor, until he died in a plane crash over Mongolia. After that, all references to Lin were banned. His image disappeared from photographs, posters, books, vases, buttons, sculptures, paintings, and all other visual manifestations of Party propaganda. Naturally, that included his words too.

Some say his plane was shot down. Others claim that the plane didn't have enough fuel. What is certain is that he had fallen out of favor with the dictator he had always served, and hailed to the end as a genius. As usual in a tyrant's court, the politics are opaque. Perhaps

Mao saw him as a potential threat to his absolute power. Perhaps Lin had been too indiscreet in his efforts to be Mao's natural successor. Perhaps the very idea of a successor reminded the Red Emperor of his own mortality, and the only way to ban such a terrible idea was to crush anyone who might come to embody it. Many men who flew too near the Chinese sun had been squashed before Lin.

Sensing his imminent downfall, Lin may have been plotting a coup of some kind. Or maybe it was his son, Lin Liguo. In any case, nothing ever came of these plans, and it is most likely that Lin tried to get away. The reason his plane probably ran out of fuel over Mongolia was because Lin's escape to the Soviet Union had been too hasty.

What makes the Little Red Book in the Library so special is that it once belonged to Lin. Not that one would know from the book's appearance—no signature, no jottings, or any other personal marks. I even held the little book to my nose, since I had read somewhere that Lin's hygienic habits left something to desire. But . . . not a whiff of anything.

The poignancy of Lin's ownership of this copy of Mao's quotations lies not only in his sad demise. It was Lin who compiled the quotations in the first place, in 1964, culled from the Chairman's speeches and writings. One of his reasons for doing this was to make the People's Liberation Army into the central organ of power in China. Military and party authority were supposed to be indistinguishable. Worship of Mao's words had to result in absolute obedience to the revolutionary armed forces. One of the most important quotations, to Lin, was: "The Chinese Red Army is an armed body for carrying out the political tasks of the revolution."

In any case, Lin became the most successful editor in history, since more than six billion copies of the book were printed in little more than a decade. He was one of the main architects of Mao's personality cult, which reached the hysterical proportions of an ultra-orthodox religion, especially during the Cultural Revolution, whose bible was the Little Red Book.

Every Chinese was required to carry the book on his or her person at all times, study it, and learn its contents by heart. Refusal, or even simply forgetting to do so, could lead to one's death. Labor was interrupted in fields and factories for lengthy study sessions of the book. Couples getting married were invariably given a copy of the book.

Some people had so many copies, they didn't know what to do with them. Pulping, or throwing them away, was of course out of the question. Chinese embassies gave out the book. It was translated into almost every language. For years, waving the book, like a magic totem, was part of mass rallies.

Like the Bible, or Hitler's *Mein Kampf,* the Little Red Book was more than a book. It was meant to be taken as holy writ. Damaging the pages of the book, stepping onto it inadvertently, getting it wet or soiled, was enough to get a person into serious trouble. Criticism, let alone ridicule, was unthinkable.

That the contents of this iconic little book were treated with deep reverence even by many people in the West, who were under no compulsion to do so, cannot have had much to do with the originality, interest, or entertainment of Mao's thoughts. For the most part, the quotations are little more than fortune cookies of the Chinese revolution: "A revolution is not a dinner party"; "Our enemies are all those in league with imperialism"; "We should support whatever the enemy opposes and oppose whatever the enemy supports." And so on, and on.

The point is not the intrinsic interest of the words. The words are revered because they were uttered by Mao. In a way, the cult of the Little Red Book is a modern perversion of the reverence for words in Confucianism. Like students of the Quran, traditional Chinese scholars had to learn the Confucian classics—compilations of moral and political sayings—by rote. A learned and virtuous man spouted quotations from Confucius in the same way Maoists recited the words of the Chairman. One major difference between the fifth-century-B.C.E. sage and the 20th-century dictator is that the former spoke in terms of tolerance, restraint, and moderation, while the latter was notable for his unabashed brutality: "Everything reactionary is the same; if you don't hit it, it won't fall. This is also like sweeping the floor; as a rule, where the broom does not reach, the dust will not vanish of itself."

Mao loathed Confucius and everything he stood for. To him, moderation was reactionary. And he believed, like many radical intellectuals of his generation, that Confucianism was the main impediment to Chinese progress. The classics were part of the "four olds," which had to be annihilated before China could move forward.

I first read Mao's writings as a student of Chinese in the early

1970s. One of the key texts we had to study in a class on modern Chinese formed part of what was called the "Criticize Lin Biao and Confucius Campaign," unleashed by Mao's ferocious wife, Jiang Qing, in 1973. The language was both hysterical and deadly dull, consisting of endless denunciations of Lin Biao's reactionary plots to restore capitalism. One of the things held against him was his effort to promote Mao as a genius, which was of course linked to his promotion of the Little Red Book.

This made no sense at all, of course, except in the paranoid world of a dying tyrant's court. The idea was that Lin, by declaiming Mao as a genius, was attempting to kick the great leader upstairs into heaven, as it were, so that Lin could take over the reigns of worldly power. The purpose of continuing to denounce Lin several years after his death was to preserve the image of Mao as the sole leader of a permanent revolution. The enemies were everywhere, symbolized by Confucius and Lin, reactionaries, revisionists, imperialists, and capitalist roaders. Only Mao would survive in this endless struggle. Lin was just one of many who were devoured by the revolution they had faithfully served. He was destroyed by the cult he had started.

A degree of sanity—call it moderation—was only restored after Mao's death. By 1979 China's new leader, Deng Xiaoping, decided that the crazier aspects of Mao's legacy had to go. And so it was decided, on February 12, 1979, by the Central Department of Propaganda that all sales of *Quotations from Chairman Mao* would be stopped forthwith. "Mao Zedong Thought," so people were told, had been "taken out of context." Lin Biao had only compiled the book "to amass political capital."

By now the Little Red Book has become a kitsch item sold in souvenir stores and street markets all over China. Most are "fakes," in the sense of having been printed long after the ban of 1979, precisely to be sold as souvenirs. Some are collector's items because of their dates or provenance. None is as valuable as the copy held in the Library, since it belonged to the man who produced it. He is long dead. And so are millions of others, who died, often horribly, in the wave of mass murder known as the Cultural Revolution. All that is left is a shabby little book in a cheap plastic cover.

毛主席语录

GABRIEL BYRNE, actor, film director, film producer, and writer

GABRIEL BYRNE

James Joyce, Paris, Berenice Abbott

gelatin silver print, 1928, Photography Collection, The Miriam and Ira D. Wallach Division of Art, Prints and Photographs

HANNAH CABELL, actor, with paperweight used by Charlotte Brontë

HANNAH CABELL

"The Keep of the Bridge," Charlotte Brontë,

holograph dated, July 13, 1829,
with two original pencil sketches,
signed and dated May 20, 1829

Charlotte Brontë has been a formative figure in my life ever since I played Jane Eyre in a stage adaptation of the novel in 2007. I hadn't read the book before I was cast, so after getting the part, I sat down to study it and was amazed. Then we toured the country with the play, performing in fifty-three cities and towns in twenty-eight states, and I was even more amazed. This story, and this character, touches people. I had heard it dismissed as "chick lit"; I wasn't sure how a mid-nineteenth-century novel would be received in small-town Georgia or the northern reaches of New York State—but there was something in this tale of a young person struggling to get through life with their dignity and soul and heart intact that did, and continues, to affect all sorts of people profoundly.

I was also fascinated by Charlotte's childhood (clearly drawn upon for Jane's experiences in the novel), and it was incredible to sit in the Library with her fairy tale, her tiny sketch, her writing desk, and the precious assorted objects she used as paperweights. I held her pencil; I read and touched a poem that she had written in 1830, years before *Jane Eyre*. As I sat there, looking at Charlotte's tiny fourteen-year-old handwriting, I was reminded of Anne Frank (whose diary I am currently immersed in, thanks to another play). I had never before thought about the parallels between these two young women: their innate talent, their driving ambition to write, their loneliness. It was a profound experience.

PETER CAREY, novelist and short story writer

PETER CAREY

VIEWING TERRY SOUTHERN

Flash and Filigree, Terry Southern
holograph manuscript

hen I arrived in New York in 1990, Terry Southern was out of print. In those long ago days, when I still went to parties that might be described as "literary," I found living legends all about me, but the writer I wanted most to meet was never among the guests. Someone told me Terry Southern was dead. Someone said that was not true. Then I met a woman who knew Terry Southern, or had, once upon a time.

"My God. What is he like?"

"He's living on road kill out on Long Island."

This was completely untrue, but I believed.

"Go and see him. He'd like to see you."

Terry Southern wanted to see me? Sure!

I did not pay my respects to Terry Southern until quite recently, when I visited The New York Public Library's Berg Collection, where a collection of his papers, a great portion of them rescued from a Chelsea mini-storage facility, had been lovingly conserved and cataloged.

It had taken years before these papers reached their safe house and a particular young man who would restore order to what one might charitably call a "dog's breakfast." In time this young librarian would become the Robert H. Taylor Curator and Department Head of Literary and Historical Manuscripts at the Morgan Library and Museum. At the time he was plain Declan Kiely. Using the resource he had available—a forty-feet-long display case and twelve months of grant money—Kiely separated the pages of different screenplays from each other, and from the novels, and the memoir notes, and the rusty paper clips, and the hundreds of lottery tickets.

I had not come all this way to see Terry Southern in a realistic light, and I was pleased not to be asked to confront the painful evidence of a once famous writer's later economic life. That is, I was spared the lottery tickets.

On December 8, 2010, in Room 320, I found the body of Terry Southern's *Flash and Filigree* had been prepared for viewing. There were three neat stacks: the final fair copy, the penultimate marked-up copy (on which the author's amendments seemed to be few and of no great importance), and finally, inside a clear plastic folder, aging sheets of fragile acid paper covered with handwriting even worse than my own. The pages of this draft seemed to be as crumbly as butterfly wings. Their age and frailty, their general unloveliness produced in me the same deep sadness I feel when coming across corals in glass cases in provincial museums. All heat had gone from the writer's pen, all its glory and its juices had disappeared. For the librarian Declan Kiely, one might imagine, this had been a pharaoh's tomb rescued from the grave robbers. But for this one writer, already in his sixties, it engendered a depressive state, thoughts of all those endless churning hours of labor, the false assumption that nothing else in life might matter, the conceit and futility of a writer's life.

In this state of high emotion, I could hardly read a word of the rescued manuscripts. I played with Southern's typewriter, examined its black ribbon, and slipped away.

As it happened I had brought a brand-new Grove paperback of *Flash and Filigree* along with me. It had fitted very snugly in the inside pocket of my heavy leather coat. Now, outside on the steps on Fifth Avenue, in the freezing New York cold, with my woolen hat pulled down across my ears, I dug out the novel and removed a glove to more easily turn its pages. The paper was new and white, the type was cold and sharp and black. I read one page, then another. I retreated from the freezing wind, against the wall, behind a pillar. It was thirty-two degrees but I had only to read seven pages to arrive at what I sought—the scene where the fastidious Treevly, a new patient, describes the long history of his lesion to Doctor Eichner. In the course of a single page it becomes weirder and weirder. He has, Treevly finally reports, introduced cancer culture into his lesion and it has "cleared up nicely."

"Yes, of course," said the Doctor and, as he spoke, standing very close, he brought the paperweight down sharply across the back of the young man's skull."

I laughed, as if I had never read the words before.

Mr Treevly crumpled, but before he could slip to the floor, Dr Eichner pushed him back onto the sofa. Then he walked rapidly to the desk, undoing the handkerchief for the paperweight and replaced it, with the clips and rubber bands, on the desk. He sat down, took a sheet of memo-paper and his pen.

My eyes were running, from laughter and the cold. I removed my glasses and pressed my sniffing nose against the page.

You are lying, he wrote. You are a psychopathic liar. If you ever come back here, I will turn you over to the police. I warn you: stay away, and leave me alone; or you will find yourself in very serious trouble—

There are some books, as we all know, that cannot live up to the certainties of our youthful enthusiasms. How sweet to discover that *Flash and Filigree* was not among them. I opened my hands and the volume rose up, transcendent in the freezing air, floating high above the lions on Fifth Avenue, releasing lottery tickets and a shower of rusty paper clips, which together fell like fairy dust amid the cell phone conversations on the steps below.

ANNE CARSON, poet, essayist, and translator

ANNE CARSON

"The Little Maid and the Gentleman, or, We Are Seven," William Wordsworth

embellished with engravings [1820?]

Depending on your view of life and death, it is a dismal little poem. Wordsworth wrote it in 1798. It is essentially a quarrel between "I" and a "little Maid" about whether the dead should be counted or not and was inspired by a real little girl he met on one of his walks. He asks about her family. She says her family includes seven children, although two of them "are in the church-yard laid." He insists this makes a sum of five, not seven. She resists his calculation throughout the seventeen stanzas of the poem. She has a gracious wild persistence about her, he seems a callous dogmatist. They rhyme in and out of each other's verses without any meeting of minds or softening of positions. He seems to grow rather annoyed. She maintains an otherworldly calm. Strange interaction. I guess she wins. And it's nice that Wordsworth allows her this. Certainly he had his own difficulties with accepting the finality of death or adapting to separations in life. Imagination was his triumph too.

The edition of this poem, shown me by Charles Carter in the Pforzheimer Collection of The New York Pubic Library, is a book small enough to fit in the palm of the hand. Each page contains a woodcut illustration of the realia mentioned in the poem—trees, ships, coffins, little girls, snowy afternoons—in the naive style of a children's book. The woodcuts are astonishingly simple and beautiful. They make you wish to enter them, to go and sit on the edge of a coffin beside the little maid and chat with her dead brother there or argue with Wordsworth. To test that border.

WE ARE SEVEN

———A SIMPLE Child,
That lightly draws its breath,
And feels its life in every limb,
What should it know of death?

I met a little cottage Girl:
She was eight years old, she said;
Her hair was thick with many a curl
That clustered round her head.

She had a rustic, woodland air,
And she was wildly clad: 10
Her eyes were fair, and very fair;
—Her beauty made me glad.

"Sisters and brothers, little Maid,
How many may you be?"
"How many? Seven in all," she said
And wondering looked at me.

"And where are they? I pray you tell."
She answered, "Seven are we;
And two of us at Conway dwell,
And two are gone to sea. 20

"Two of us in the church-yard lie,
My sister and my brother;
And, in the church-yard cottage, I
Dwell near them with my mother."

"You say that two at Conway dwell,
And two are gone to sea,
Yet ye are seven!—I pray you tell,
Sweet Maid, how this may be."

Then did the little Maid reply,
"Seven boys and girls are we; 30
Two of us in the church-yard lie,
Beneath the church-yard tree."

"You run about, my little Maid,
Your limbs they are alive;
If two are in the church-yard laid,
Then ye are only five."

"Their graves are green, they may be seen,"
The little Maid replied,
"Twelve steps or more from my mother's door,
And they are side by side. 40

"My stockings there I often knit,
My kerchief there I hem;
And there upon the ground I sit,
And sing a song to them.

"And often after sunset, Sir,
When it is light and fair,
I take my little porringer,
And eat my supper there.

"The first that died was sister Jane;
In bed she moaning lay, 50
Till God released her of her pain;
And then she went away.

"So in the church-yard she was laid;
And, when the grass was dry,
Together round her grave we played,
My brother John and I.

"And when the ground was white with snow,
And I could run and slide,
My brother John was forced to go,
And he lies by her side." 60

"How many are you, then," said I,
"If they two are in heaven?"
Quick was the little Maid's reply,
"O Master! we are seven."

"But they are dead; those two are dead!
Their spirits are in heaven!"
'Twas throwing words away; for still
The little Maid would have her will,
And said, "Nay, we are seven!"

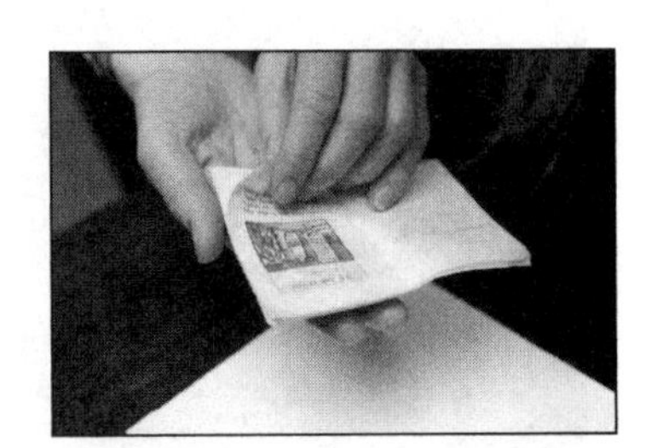

CHARLES CUYKENDALL CARTER, bibliographer, The Carl H. Pforzheimer Collection of Shelley and His Circle

CHARLES CARTER

Frankenstein, or the Modern Prometheus,
Mary Wollstonecraft Shelley

1818

ary Shelley's *Frankenstein* testifies to the powers of a young mind. Its author was, famously, only eighteen when she began writing it. To some, a teenage girl crafting such an enduring piece of fiction may seem as likely as a crazed scientist infusing a patchwork of corpses with the spark of life. Mary Shelley's genius was not, however, concocted through arcane sciences; it had the encouragement of her father—the writer William Godwin—and was sustained by open admission to his impressive library.

Access to books helped foster Mary's intellectual curiosity and dedication to writing. She was lucky. Most children—especially girls—in early-nineteenth-century England (and America) didn't have much choice in their reading materials. It's hard for us to imagine, because for the last hundred years, The New York Public Library has provided free access to countless works that have fueled lifelong learning and creativity in millions of people in our communities. Doubtless, today the Library is facilitating inspiration for Mary Shelleys of the future.

The Pforzheimer Collection holds three copies of the first edition of *Frankenstein*. Though each is precious, I'm particularly fond of the one in its original boards—quite attractive, pink mottled boards—with the original spine labels. Its singular characteristic, unfortunately omitted from most later editions, is a full-page dedication that reads: "To William Godwin . . . these volumes are respectfully inscribed by the author."

GRAYDON CARTER, editor of *Vanity Fair*

GRAYDON CARTER

LIFE BEGINS AT 8:30

Daily Menu 9/3/1966

Ye Waverly Inn at 16 Bank Street,
corner of Waverly Place, New York

It's something of a delight to discover that three of the principal joys of the manly arts—smoking, drinking, and eating—are represented in an institution as temperate and august as New York's beloved Public Library. Imagine stumbling into your favorite watering hole and discovering that all the pastimes that you once cherished have escaped the clutches of probity and intolerance and are back and in glorious flower. For if there is anything aside from pure historical scholarship that tells us what it was like to live back when, it is the trappings of pure enjoyment. And if there is a single document that harks back to those long-frowned-upon pleasures, it is the restaurant menu. History is most surely made at night.

The Library has no fewer than 40,000 menus in its Rare Book Division, the result of a bequest made by a woman with the curious name Miss Frank E. Buttolph. Before the current library was even built, she had donated her own collection and then spent much of the next quarter century adding to it—indeed it became her life.

Many of the menus benefit by being produced during golden ages of typography and illustration—and in at least one instance, of train travel as well. There is a charming mid-century children's menu for the New Haven Railroad, once owned by Morgans and Mellons, that is die-cut in the shape of a circus elephant. It allows its small diners to order by jungle animal, each of which is represented by a silhouette. The "Monkey," for example, offers creamed chicken on toast, mashed potatoes, fresh vegetables, Horlick's malted milk, and vanilla ice cream—all for 70 cents.

Every type of establishment is represented here, from the palaces of high consumption, such as Delmonico's and Le Pavillion, to louche dining and drinking spots, such as Trader Vic's and the Waverly Inn. In the early '30s, the latter was owned by the secretary to then *Vanity Fair* managing editor Claire Boothe. And in a circuitous bit of happenstance, I am one of its owners now.

The Waverly's menu from September 1966 is an elegant but simple affair. About nine inches square, it is folded in half and has a length of string with a tassel at the end holding it together at the spine. There is a watercolor illustration of the restaurant and the simple, Federal-style, mid-nineteenth-century brownstones running west toward the Hudson River. A new menu was typed every day and then copied in a pre-Xerox fashion known as mimeograph that old-timers will remember for its light blue type, and that, when fresh from the machine, gave off a heavenly, evocative smell. The sheet was then slipped in behind the red string. The phone number was listed as CHelsea 3-0396.

Dishes and prices reflect the appetites of the time, as well as the pocketbooks. Hawaiian chicken over rice and Chinese noodles was listed at $2.85. And chicken pot pie, a longtime Waverly Inn standby, was then just $2.75. It came with vegetables, a green salad, and rice or mashed potatoes. The pot pie is still on the menu. And aside from the prices, not much else has changed. Indeed the houses along the block in the illustration look the same, including the one a few doors down where I live. It is a place where smoking, drinking, and eating are still very much permitted.

ROSANNE CASH, singer, songwriter, essayist, and author

ROSANNE CASH

Original Pen and India Ink Drawings by Rockwell Kent

from *Moby-Dick, or, The Whale* by Herman Melville
1930 edition

Leaves of Grass by Walt Whitman

Brooklyn, 1855

"Passage to India," Walt Whitman

autograph manuscript, 1869

I can't go down Fifth Avenue and pass by the elegant facade and the stone lions of the Library without remembering that there was once a reservoir there. Now the vast reading rooms, the floors upon floors of stacks and archives, the sweeping staircases and the little side rooms stuffed with arcane and wonderful artifacts, maps and photographs, are a reservoir of our history, our humanity, our great ideas and deepest feelings, our attention to detail, our obsessions, our follies, and our intellectual redemption.

Shortly after I moved to New York in 1991, I went to the Library to peruse the passenger lists of nineteenth-century ships to see if I could find my mother's ancestors. I found them, a little group of adventurers, huddled together at the bottom of the manifest of a ship that sailed from Palermo, Sicily, into New York Harbor in the pre–Ellis Island era. It was thrilling to find a piece of my own deep history there, waiting for me to discover it, in my Library, my New York, my home.

No less exciting was my most recent visit to the Library, where I was guided into a hidden, wood-paneled room on an upper floor and allowed to hold an original copy of Walt Whitman's *Leaves Of Grass,* as well as some of his original manuscript pages of his poem "Passage to India," corrected, revised, and scratched up by the man himself. My eyes unexpectedly and suddenly welled with tears while holding the book, and, horrified, I realized that my postmodern tears were on the verge of staining the prototype of "Song of Myself." I sniffed with fierce resolve, and, thankfully, *Leaves of Grass* remains unsullied.

The same afternoon, in the gorgeous Rare Map Room, I pored over a magnificent mid-nineteenth-century map of my own neighborhood of Chelsea, and found listings of "insalubrious" houses, as well as houses where yellow fever had been diagnosed. The vast property belonging to Clement Clarke Moore, the gentleman who wrote "The Night Before Christmas," was clearly demarcated, just three blocks from where I live. The little wood cottages on the river, now the huge complex of Chelsea Piers, were carefully and individually drawn. Whitman, long before finishing *Leaves of Grass,* lived in one of those cottages for a time and worked on the docks. Studying just this one small section of one map of the New York of 160 years ago was both a history lesson, with a happy peripheral connection to the Whitman book I had just left upstairs, and a real moment of time travel.

I don't imagine I will ever see even a tenth of what the Library has to offer. But each time I go, I'm led to some specific artifact, book, or era that transports me for an afternoon, that allows me to time-travel and dream and learn. I can't see and feel it all, but I can go to this reservoir of beauty and knowledge again and again, and find parts of myself, past and future, and sustenance for my present mind and spirit.

RON CHERNOW, biographer

RON CHERNOW

Washington's Farewell Address, September 1796

George Washington papers, 1694-1932

The New York Public Library has a fantastic set of original documents that enables us to chart the entire evolution of Washington's Farewell Address. Mind you, of all the documents to emerge from the founding era, this one is superseded in importance only by the Declaration of Independence and the U.S. Constitution. So this document rates as something close to American scripture, part of the grand canon of influential writings of the founding era. In this address, which was meant to be read and not spoken, Washington issued a stirring plea for national unity; warned of the perils of partisan politics—a timely message that still resonates with us today; and urged Americans in the future to avoid permanent political alliances with other countries, although he did support commercial alliances.

This document has achieved such iconic status—it's read on the floor of the U.S. Senate every year—that Americans tend to imagine that it came from Washington's hands perfectly chiseled in marble. But as the documents at The New York Public Library attest, it had a very long and complicated history. Washington had considered resigning at the end of his first term and had asked James Madison to draft the first farewell address. One crisis after another then supervened and Washington decided to serve a second term. In the final year of that second term, he asked Alexander Hamilton both to revise Madison's draft and to prepare a brand-new version, if he were so inclined. Washington ended up preferring Hamilton's version, so that the latter emerged as the principal wordsmith of the Farewell Address, although that was a fairly well-kept secret for many years. Hamilton used to laugh whenever people tried to sell him copies of the Farewell Address on the streets of New York.

How splendid and quite extraordinary that The New York Public Library contains Madison's first draft of the farewell address, one of Hamilton's letters of commentary on the address, and then the finished version for which Hamilton was the principal ghostwriter. These papers therefore allow us to eavesdrop on the very process of creation, so that what can seem like a timeless document turns into a very human en-deavor, full of changes and compromises and refinements. We're able to enter into the very workshop where history is made. This is what historical research should be all about: a behind-the-scenes look at history's great moments, where we see the hesitations and false starts and then, as in this case, the miraculously beautiful final results.

DAVID CHRISTIE, print specialist, The Miriam and Ira D. Wallach Division of Art, Prints and Photographs

DAVID CHRISTIE

The Temptation of St. Anthony, Martin Schongauer
engraving, 1470s, Print Collection, Miriam and Ira D. Wallach Division of Art, Prints and Photographs

---

I love this engraving by Martin Schongauer for the extremes of emotion and exertion that it portrays. St. Anthony is the calm center in a swirl of agitated demons that has borne him aloft. His expression, beleaguered yet patient, plays counterpoint to the vigorously distorted faces of his tormentors, and his balanced poise contrasts with their wild contortions. I love and appreciate Schongauer's creativity in the conception of these monsters, having recombined to fantastic effect features of the observed natural world, such as skin, scales, spikes, and feathers. As a print lover, I am also enchanted by Schongauer's masterful technique. At a point when engraving was a relatively new pictorial art, Schongauer expanded the graphic vocabulary of the medium with a wondrous variety of long and short lines, dots, flecks, and curves to evoke the assorted textures of rough hides, feathered wings, wiry fur, and silky human hair. This print was duly famous in its time, and—being small, portable, and produced in multiples—its influence ranged as far as Italy, where Michelangelo was inspired to create a vividly colored painting based on it.

STEPHEN COLBERT, political satirist, writer, comedian, and host of *The Colbert Report*

STEPHEN COLBERT

J.D. Salinger Letters—*The New Yorker* Records

ca. 1924–1984

I suspect this photo would have annoyed J.D. Salinger. Here I am, the stereotypical liberal arts fanboy, going weak over something he typed.

But I can't help myself. When I first read Salinger, I thought he wrote the Glass family stories just for me. In the Library's Manuscript and Archives Division, I read one letter in which he worried that readers would think Franny was pregnant—he doesn't think she is, but can't be sure. I found this uncertainty about his own characters comforting. I (and I suspect many readers) felt that Salinger cheated me out of all the stories of Boo Boo and Waker and Walt and Zooey and Franny and Buddy and Seymour that I so desperately wanted. But the fact that he doesn't know (and says in the letter that he can never know) all about them, somehow blunts my resentment. These characters had their own stories and their own lives, into which both we and Salinger had only a small window. To different degrees, that puts us in the same boat.

I'm so happy that I got to see these letters and original manuscripts. Make an appointment, and so can you.

KATHRYN COURT, president and publisher of Penguin Books

KATHRYN COURT

Mr. William Shakespeares Comedies, Histories & Tragedies

First Folio Edition, 1623

y first encounter with The New York Public Library was on a visit to the city in the early 1970s at the beginning of a trip by bus across America. It left a very strong impression on me, partly because the building was so beautiful, but more importantly because it was a truly democratic institution, open to anyone who wanted to come to read, to study, to write. To my knowledge, there is nothing else quite like it anywhere in the world. Over the years, I have learned that is the repository of many extraordinary collections, among them the Berg Collection, home to a First Folio edition of Shakespeare's plays, published in 1623. Out of the original 1,000 copies that were printed, only 228 are still in existence, and I had never seen a copy before. It's hard to describe my feelings on opening that volume containing thirty-six of the most brilliant plays ever written, but it underlined how privileged we New Yorkers are to have the Library's riches at our fingertips.

ELIZABETH CAMPBELL DENLINGER, curator, The Carl H. Pforzheimer Collection of Shelley and His Circle

ELIZABETH C. DENLINGER

Baxter's Sussex Pocket Book

1810

The full title of the object I've chosen is *Baxter's Sussex pocket book . . . for the year 1810. Containing useful particulars of the county . . . Also ruled pages for memorandums and cash account adapted for every week in the year. Illustrated with a neat map of the county* (Lewes: Sussex Press, 1810).

In selecting a favorite object from the collection, I had a much smaller than usual pool to draw from. At the moment of this writing (February 2011), most of the treasures of Shelley and his circle are on display at Oxford's Bodleian Library in an exhibition called *Shelley's Ghost,* which will arrive at NYPL in February 2012. *The Esdaile Notebook,* the holograph revisions to *Queen Mab,* the manuscript of *A Philosophical View of Reform*—all are abroad.

So I've chosen this red leather diary that Shelley kept fitfully during his last term at Eton. One scholar has speculated that Shelley's father, hoping to teach fiscal prudence, had him keep accounts in it. There are also references to *Zastrozzi* and *St. Irvyne,* Gothic novels Shelley published while still a schoolboy, and plans to play hooky with his fellow Etonians. The most poignant item is a lock of hair tucked into the diary's pocket. Held together by sealing wax and impressed with a rebus denoting "I expect a return" (of hair? affection? or both?), it is from Shelley's early love, his cousin Harriet Grove. The spring of 1810 saw the flowering of their love, but her family disapproved and she broke it off in the autumn of that year.

KIRAN DESAI, writer

KIRAN DESAI

Shiohi no tsuto or *Gifts of the Ebb Tide*
(known as The Shell Book), Kitagawa Utamaro
polychrome woodblock prints,
undated probably 1789, Spencer Collection

JIM DINE, artist and poet

JIM DINE

A recording of Robert Creeley

The Spoken Arts Treasury of 100 Modern American Poets,
vol. 16, Spoken Arts 1978

Last week I went to The New York Public Library for the Performing Arts to listen to my dead friend Robert Creeley read his poems. To have him back in my ears thrilled me and once again informed how his poems should be heard. For me, this branch of the Library on Amsterdam Avenue and 65th Street became a source of magic and memory.

NATHAN ENGLANDER, writer

NATHAN ENGLANDER

Hunt-Lenox Globe

ca. 1510

Back in 2004, I was basically living at The New York Public Library. With a novel to finish and a Cullman Center Fellowship that gave me unrestricted access to the building, I was working at the Library day and night. When I needed to untangle some idea, I'd head upstairs to the Edna Barnes Salomon Room, which was being used as a gallery of the Library's treasures. I'd go stare at the idyllic Asher B. Durand painting *Kindred Spirits,* or study the Gutenberg Bible through glass. I spent a lot of time standing under a giant Munkácsy painting, a dark oil whose title translates as "Blind Milton dictating *Paradise Lost* to his daughters." It is, as described, a portrait of the author—sightless—dictating his masterpiece. I'd look up at Milton holding forth to his daughters and, dead seriously, I'd tell myself, "That man finished his book blind, now get back to work!"

Even greater than the push Milton gave me, there was one piece in that room that truly inspired. Along with the Bible, the first thing one would see when stepping into the Salomon Room was a stunning metal globe. The globe, which dates from around 1510, is the oldest engraved copper sphere in existence with a depiction of the New World. Called the Hunt-Lenox Globe, it's one of the Library's most precious artifacts.

If one looks at the Western Hemisphere on the Hunt-Lenox, North America simply isn't. The continent of South America is pictured as a large island. I can't tell you how much time I spent admiring it. That representation of South America was, to me, a thing of great beauty.

At the time, I was a half dozen years into writing a novel set in Argentina. Busy building my own South America, I was completely taken with this other vision of that place. Here was an anonymous cartographer's alternate truth—one that, like fiction, was founded partially on dreams. Staring at the globe's South America and knowing, logically, that it was completely wrong, I couldn't ever—looking at its concreteness, taken in by its beauty—see it as anything but right. And I took that lesson very seriously. Here was one version of a world dreamed into reality and standing in harmony with another. And I'd think, the Hunt-Lenox has its South America and I'll have mine.

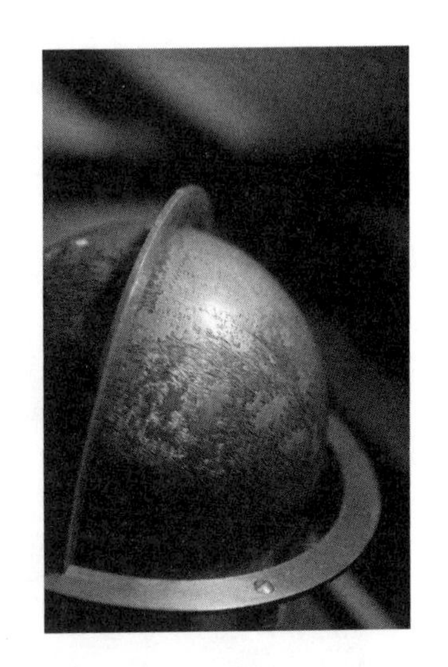

WILL ENO, playwright

WILL ENO

Unidentified Baseball Player with Mustache, James Wallace Black

albumen print, ca. 1928, Photography Collection
The Miriam and Ira D. Wallach Division of Art,
Prints and Photographs

Back when the backyard was the world and everywhere else was far away, I had, like almost everyone else of my height and weight, a baseball card collection. It was only a few dozen cards, none that special, and in no particular order, but it was something real to have and hold, something to refer to when it was raining or my arm was broken. It's long lost and was lost so well that I couldn't even tell you what decade it got lost in. I'm sure it was one. Over the years, physics, in a funny way, has ridden to the rescue and given some solace with the fact that matter cannot be created or destroyed. Maybe *solace* isn't the word. But we can be sure that my baseball cards, along with all of your lost but once beloved things, are, according to one of the laws we have to obey, in some shape or form, somewhere. Everything else must be more or less somewhere too.

A very small but real percentage of everything, a thin but intricate and crucial slice of it, is in the collections of The New York Public Library. And the beautiful thing is that it all got there on purpose, or, through the exactly right series of accidents. It got there, in some measure, in some form, through love. Care is somewhere at the bottom of all of this. Every prominent document, every tapestry and map, or cigar box or menu, is there in the Library because it was, at some point, someone's great happiness, some breathing person's joy, a thing about which he or she would say, "You have to come look at this."

We all have our grand plans for the future and we easily imagine our name over a wing in every hospital and library, but really, a collection begins when we don't throw something away. Think of The New York Public Library as a residential home, after the owner has died. Imagine a visitor from another planet sifting through its collections, the way we might do at an estate sale, where we're saddened and gladdened and surprised at all the things that people save. Imagine this alien creature holding up a medieval medical illustration and calling to her alien boyfriend, "Hey, look! It's another one of these."

Humanity has its troubles and drawbacks, of course, but when you look at the things we cherish and save, we all seem very dear, very clumsy and life-sized. It's in this context, or one very like it, that I would like to highlight, from the A.G. Spalding Baseball Collection, "Unidentified baseball player with mustache, Boston." I do this partly as a Boston fan, and partly as a fan of anonymity. You would think, in the past couple hundred years, someone would've figured out his name. If efforts have been made, he has resisted and remains nameless, or, named, in a way, but named only by an archivist. It's worthwhile to wonder whether the world could ever get so disorganized and misfiled that we might one day look at a photo of Luciano Pavarotti, titled "Unknown singer with beard." Unlikely, but give it a thousand years, a few earthquakes, a worldwide flu epidemic or two. This is the sort of time frame and tragic lens it's hard not to see things through when you're at the Library.

That this little card kept making the cut, kept not getting lost, and now is housed in the collection for however long perpetuity is going to last has to make you feel good about the world of things, the world of people. It doesn't have to make you feel good, on second thought, but it can. Obviously it's difficult and complicated. There is a very sweet and seemingly pointless side to the long march of history. There is also a pretty rough and pointed side, in which meaning is created and destroyed on a daily basis, in a daily way. Perspective is one of the things we can hope for.

So, by all means, be sure to stop by the Declaration of Independence, in Thomas Jefferson's own human handwriting. Enjoy the Japanese erotica and make sure to see the first letter home from Christopher Columbus. There's a Gutenberg Bible, some illuminated Hebrew manuscripts, and the thoughts of Chairman Mao. There are wildly historical things to be seen.

Just don't forget that there was also once, and still remains in some way, an unknown man with a mustache, standing in the sun, playing baseball. He undoubtedly tore muscles and had questions about his knees. Possibly he had a drinking problem or two. Maybe he thought about writing a book or owning a restaurant. It's mid-July, in an earlier century, and he's alive in history. And he's deep in center field, backpedaling, tracking a long fly ball, going, going, with no idea of what the future holds. He's drifting back, he's fading back, he's at the fence. All eyes are on the ball. A woman in a sundress is reaching up with one hand and trying to keep the fancy hat on her head with the other.

REBECCA FEDERMAN, electronic resources coordinator and culinary collections, Collections Strategy Division

REBECCA FEDERMAN

Recipes [for the] United States Army, Navy, Air Force, and Marine Corps

United States. Dept. of Defense
1969. From the General Research Division

JAMES FENTON, poet, journalist, and literary critic

JAMES FENTON

"The Waste Land," T. S. Eliot

typescript with the author's manuscript corrections, unsigned and undated

ore or less from the time of its first publication, in 1922, T.S. Eliot's "The Waste Land" was recognized as the most significant poem, in English, in its era. You could argue about its merits. Indeed it almost invited mockery and parody. But such hostile or baffled attention as it received only reinforced the sense of its importance. Anyhow the admirers could be as baffled as the critics: there was a revolutionary power here that could not be ignored, and those poets who decided that, despite everything, they would continue to plough the same furrow as before, did so with a kind of self-consciousness that came from their refusal to take Eliot's lead. It is also the case—but this is a different point—that the *manuscript* of "The Waste Land" is one of the most fascinating poetry manuscripts of its era. Other great documents—for instance the papers of Wilfred Owen—show us, over the course of their revisions, how a poet comes to make those decisions and revisions that distinguish a promising, or not so promising, line from a great one. Owen writes:

> "O Jesus Christ!" one fellow sighed
> And kneeled, and bowed, tho' not in prayer, and died.

Then he finds this too wordy, and he replaces it with a single line: "'Oh! Jesus Christ! I'm hit,' he said, and died." Between the first and the final version you can feel a poet coming into his own.

"The Waste Land" manuscript has this fascination, but is notable in another way. It was talked about well before it became generally known to have survived, and the reason why it was talked about was that it was believed by the admirers of Eliot and Ezra Pound that Pound, the dedicatee of the poem, *il miglior fabbro*, the "better craftsman," had been responsible in no small measure for its success. Pound, the noisy and opinionated, tireless promoter of modern poetry, had taken something reputedly incoherent and made it cohere. "The Waste Land" was Eliot's success, but it was a triumph of Pound's editing.

Today Pound appears rather less of a figure than he did when I was coming of age, when it was common to find among one's friends and contemporaries people for whom Pound was the hero, the central proponent of modernism. Now before we get to his virtues, we have to take a long, sobering look at his faults. But in those days, although many of the faults were perfectly well known, there seemed to be a way of putting them on one side, as something to be tackled at some time in the future. Meanwhile, if you looked at the shelves of anyone seriously interested in poetry, you would expect to find at least the *Pisan Cantos* and *The ABC of Reading*. This too was what found its way into the backpacks of the enthusiasts.

To a great extent, when it was eventually published in facsimile in 1971, edited by Eliot's widow, Valerie Eliot, the manuscript of "The Waste Land" confirmed what the Poundians had claimed. The key to Pound's editing had been the preparedness to cut, and to cut fearlessly. Whole sections just went under the knife. The reason why the fourth section of the eventual poem, "Death by Water," was so much shorter than the others turned out to be that Pound had just cut everything else away. Nor have I ever seen it argued that Pound cut too much, or that beautiful passages were sacrificed. It really seems as if Pound understood Eliot as well as Eliot understood himself, or better.

Eliot could be self-deprecating in his sly way, when talking about "The Waste Land," and he seems to have enjoyed giving the impression that there was less to it than met the eye:

> *Various critics have done me the honour to interpret the poem in terms of criticism of the contemporary world, have consid-*

ered it, indeed, as an important bit of social criticism. To me it was only the relief of a personal and wholly insignificant grouse against life; it is just a piece of rhythmical grumbling.

I take this as being disingenuous. Nevertheless, I can see that it reflects a memory of that time in the poet's life when he was recovering from a nervous breakdown, in Margate and Lausanne. And I can see that in such a state of mind Eliot might indeed have been very far from clear what the purpose and plan of his poem was to be.

Techniques of cut-and-paste that today form a basic part of the skills of a writer, composer, or painter would have baffled contemporary readers. The manuscript shows us that Pound was not baffled at all. He had a strong and unerring instinct for what Eliot was after. And here it is, the jottings, the typed pages with their manuscript comments, the different hands at work on the uncertain result, each flimsy page in its transparent sleeve: offering us one kind of key to a poem which, its early readers thought, was itself a key to the age in which they were living.

RENÉE FLEMING, soprano and musical ambassador

RENÉE FLEMING

"Psyché," Emile Paladilhe

holograph, 1844

I've made a career of singing pieces that are off the beaten track of standard repertoire. When I first started performing, this was a novelty, but now more and more of us want to explore the hidden corners of the musical universe. The New York Public Library for the Performing Arts is a fantastic place to discover that material.

I used the Library constantly when I was a Juilliard student, not least because I was inspired by the incredible collection of performances that is here. Whether in recording, or video, or on DVD, to be able to actually see the performance—long after the curtains have drawn closed—is an extraordinary thing for an artist. Our artistic lives are so fleeting, and a singer in particular has perhaps a twenty-year career, so to be able to hear a voice that's never going to be heard again, and to see that person onstage, is a particular gift to be treasured.

I love musical manuscripts as well. They inspire us because we feel closer to the composer: the equivalent of a handwritten letter, only far more complex. Can you imagine orchestrating something, or setting down on paper in a legible fashion what one hundred instruments would play, potentially at the same time as a chorus? It's incredible.

The Library's long list of beautiful manuscripts is overwhelming, but I selected "Psyché" by Paladilhe because it is a song that I have loved since I was a child. My mother used it with her students. I was immediately attracted to the clarity and evocative nature of the writing, and it was a thrill to eventually record it myself. It's interesting that my daughter then decided, without any encouragement from me, that she wanted to learn it as well. I guess there must just be something intrinsically beautiful about a song that can immediately capture three generations!

JONATHAN FRANZEN, novelist, essayist, and journalist

JONATHAN FRANZEN

The Birds of America, John James Audubon
1st ed.

Although I love birds and America, I've never been a fan of John James Audubon. I know he was important historically, but the songbirds in smaller reproductions of his paintings seem wan and lifeless in comparison to the blazingly bright bundles of energy that I can see in American trees or fields with my binoculars. Audubon worked in an age before binoculars, which meant that the only way that he could see most species at close range was to kill them. His birds—especially the little tree dwellers, whose natural poses were impossible for him to see in detail—therefore often look droopy and overstretched, their heads lolling at dead-animal angles. They bear an unfortunate resemblance to the dulled, diminished bird specimens you see mounted in museums.

So I was not prepared, when I visited the Library as part of this anthology project, for the splendor of the first edition of *The Birds of America*. In a unique circumstance, four of the Library's founding pillars—Robert Leighton Stuart, James Lenox, John Jacob Astor, and Samuel J. Tilden—had copies of the book's four volumes in their private libraries or collections and gave them to the Library. The volume I saw was nearly the size of a single bed and required teamwork to turn its pages, and as soon as we turned to the first illustration I realized that I'd been mistaken about Audubon. The engraving work was gorgeous, and the colors, all hand-painted, were still incredibly vivid. Even the little birds, when seen as they were meant to be seen, were full not only of life but also of the love with which Audubon had painted them.

I was particularly moved by the illustration of Carolina parakeets. This bird, the only parrot native to eastern North America, became extinct early in the twentieth century. The causes of its extinction were various: clearing of the great forests in which they nested, hunting by farmers who considered them a pest, capture and killing for the pet and millinery trades, and, perhaps, competition with introduced European honeybees for nest cavities. What made the parakeets exceptionally vulnerable to hunting was their sociability. When a hunter shot one of them, the rest of the flock, instead of fleeing to safety, came crowding to the aid of the fallen bird, exposing themselves to further shots. To wipe out an entire flock, all you had to do was kill one bird.

As befits the parakeets' social nature, Audubon's painting shows seven of them crowded together in a tangle of branches, three of them with open beaks, one of them seeming about to fly directly at the viewer, and all of them angled to show off their intensely green wing and tail plumage and their gold-and-red heads. Nobody will ever see these birds alive again, but they were alive in a book in the Library, more energetic and natural in their poses than almost any other bird that Audubon painted. I was left to imagine that the reason they looked so natural was that Audubon had had an unusually good opportunity to study their postures at close range, after he'd shot the first of them.

JONATHAN GALASSI, president and publisher of Farrar, Straus and Giroux, translator, and poet

JONATHAN GALASSI

Poems, May 1927–March 1929, W.H. Auden

holograph notebook, signed

Poring over W.H. Auden's early poems in his copybooks at the Berg Collection was one of the most exciting reading experiences I've had in years. Auden, for me, is among the absolute greats of the past century, perhaps the greatest poet of the generation that followed the first-wave Modernists. In the notebooks from the late 1920s you see the young schoolmaster, himself barely an adult, applying the lessons he'd learned from Eliot and his cohorts to compose the clearest, crispest, most cold-eyed, woundingest love poems of the century. And to think that he wrote them in pencil! Auden was notoriously untidy in life, but he has an unwaveringly elegant hand here. The cool beauty of his lines echoes in his majestically modulated penmanship.

Take, for instance, the brilliant early lyric "The Secret Agent," written in early 1928, when the poet was just twenty-one:

Control of the passes was, he saw, the key
To this new district, but who would get it?
He, the trained spy, had walked into the trap
For a bogus guide, seduced by the old tricks.

At Greenhearth was a fine site for a dam
And easy power, had they pushed the rail

Some stations nearer. They ignored his wires:
The bridges were unbuilt and trouble coming.

The street music seemed gracious now to one
For weeks up in the desert. Woken by water
Running away in the dark, he often had
Reproached the night for a companion
Dreamed of already. They would shoot, of course,
Parting easily two that were never joined.

The Berg notebook contains several versions of this sonnet—all in Auden's error-free hand. Studying how the poem was funneled into its final shape is an intense aesthetic and intellectual pleasure that only a denizen of a sacred place like the Berg can have.

Auden became a New Yorker after he left England for America in 1939, living here intermittently until he returned to the U.K. in 1972, shortly before his death the following year. The Berg's impressive holdings include manuscripts of poems, essays and lectures, translations, and librettos, as well as letters, photographs, and memorabilia—including the certificate of the poet's marriage to Thomas Mann's daughter, Erika, on June 15, 1935. The notebook I was devouring, though, belonged to the English Auden, as Edward Mendelson and others have called him—the implacable political and sexual radical who somehow metamorphosed over time into the conservative Anglican of his last years.

The controlled lyricism of Auden's fluent, almost ethereal penmanship somehow embodies the lustrous, magnificent perfection of his obsidian lines. These early lyrics are among the poems I'm most admiring and envious of, and reading them in the flesh, as it were, is not only an unforgettable thrill—it's a unique kind of personal encounter that reveals much about the poems—and about the poet who made them—that can't be seen in a book or on a screen.

MARGARET GLOVER, librarian, The Spencer Collection

MARGARET GLOVER

Plate 3 from *Revolving Doors*, Man Ray
pochoir, 1926, Print Collection,
Miriam and Ira D. Wallach Division of
Art, Prints and Photographs

BARBARA GOLDSMITH, writer and historian

BARBARA GOLDSMITH

Alice's Adventures in Wonderland
Charles Lutwidge Dodgson (Lewis Carroll)
1865, 1st ed. and 1866, 2nd ed., presentation copy inscribed from the author to Alice Pleasance Liddell

---

I was ten. What had started as a sore throat had devolved into scarlet fever (immunization and penicillin where not yet in common use). Flushed bright red, armpits burning, isolated save for a nurse and mother, both wearing masks, I hardly knew myself. Instead of my biking-riding, friend-filled life, I sat in bed day after day reading. But the only books I remember now are *Alice's Adventures in Wonderland* and *Through the Looking-Glass.* Alice provided an escape into a fantasy world, yet one not dissimilar emotionally to the world into which I felt I had fallen. Like Alice I asked myself, "I wonder if I've been changed in the night?"

I remember putting my hand over the exemplary John Tenniel illustrations so I could picture my own Alice, a gangly girl with dark brown hair, braids, and glasses. In short, me. I remember crying when, upon my recovery, my mother wary of contamination, on the doctor's orders, burned all the books I had read and even the sheets on my bed. That illness, however, left me with a love of reading that led to writing. As Lewis Carroll observed, "If you don't know where you are going, any road will take you there." A.S. Byatt wrote that the Alice books have, "Attracted logicians, literary critics, psychoanalytic critics, theorists of childhood, experts on children's literature, biographical interpreters, imitators, and a whole host of what in Shakespearean criticism are known as Baconians and Disintegrators."

Personally, as an adult, I have rediscovered my joy in this remarkable work. I still ponder the tongue twisters, riddles, and mathematical queries posed therein by an author who was not only a skilled fabulist but also a maddening mathematician. Like Alice my math was abominable, "Let me see: four times five is twelve, and four times six is thirteen, and four times seven is—oh dear! I shall never get to twenty at that rate!" says Alice. As to my days, there are many when I hear the Red Queen saying, "It takes all the running you can do, to keep in the same place. If you want to get somewhere else, you must run at least twice as fast as that!"

As someone who lives in a world of words, I think often of Alice's exchange with the March Hare when he tells her, "You should say what you mean," and Alice replies, "I do at least—at least I mean what I say—that's the same thing, you know." "Not the same thing a bit!" replies the disgruntled Hare, "Why, you might just as well say that, I see what I eat is the same as I eat what I see . . . You might just as well say that I like what I get is the same thing as I get what I like!"

Imagine my delight in finding that in the unsurpassed Henry W. and Albert A. Berg Collection of English and American Literature at The New York Public Library there are first editions (1865 and 1866) of both *Alice's Adventures in Wonderland* and *Through the Looking-Glass* written by the mathematician and photographer Charles Lutwidge Dodgson, under the pseudonym of Lewis Carroll. The Berg Collection also possesses the original drawings for the Alice illustrations by the masterful John Tenniel, the ones I had spurned in my youth. There are photographs of Alice Pleasance Liddell, for whom the book was written, as a proper Victorian child but also as a beggar-maid, albeit in a flattering rag costume made of silk. Although she does not have braids or glasses, I noted that Alice does have dark brown hair. The photographs of Alice, her sister, Lorina (three years older than Alice), and their friends are full of life and spunk. My favorite piece of Alice ephemera in the Berg Collection is a miniature of Tweedledum and Tweedledee carved from a single piece of ivory.

The Berg Collection is a treasure chest of 35,000 printed items and a staggering 115,000 manuscripts, ranging from 1480 to the present.

It includes many of my favorite poets and writers—Elizabeth Barrett Browning, T.S. Eliot, Emily Dickinson, Charles Dickens, Joseph Conrad, Henry James, Mark Twain, Vladimir Nabokov, Paul Auster—Oh gosh, one could go on and on. But why? Go see for yourself.

Holly Golightly, the heroine of Truman Capote's *Breakfast at Tiffany's.* says that on those terrible "mean red days," she heads for Tiffany's. "It calms me down right away, the quietness and the proud look of it." But I say, my *Breakfast at Tiffany's* is The New York Public Library.

ALVARO GONZALEZ-LAZO, print specialist, The Miriam and Ira D. Wallach Division of Art, Prints and Photographs

ALVARO GONZALEZ-LAZO

Melencolia I, Albrecht Dürer

engraving, 1514, Print Collection, Miriam and Ira D. Wallach Division of Art, Prints and Photographs

ADAM GOPNIK, writer, essayist, and commentator

ADAM GOPNIK

MENUS

Menu, Le Restaurant Français

New York's World Fair, 1939

The menu ought not to be so prepossessing. What could be sadder, what could be of less use or reach, of less significance in the world, than a century-old carte from a long-closed swill shop? We ought to feel, at best, a sort of nostalgic reach when we see them—for prices that are no longer available, meals no longer to be eaten, dishes no longer made, at restaurants that no longer exist. What was once the card that they handed you to begin a journey to romance, or gluttony anyway, is now just an old, yellowed foldout with a gravy stain. *Eheu fugaces* indeed; who needs memories of meals we never ate at prices that they no longer offer?

And yet when I look at menus in The New York Public Library—or see them on the walls of the collection—I feel just the opposite. I feel a high-hearted burst of pleasure, even of possibility, though knowing that the actual possibilities were foreclosed long ago. No papers give more pleasure; I would trade Aspern and all *his* papers for one saved menu from an inn where he stopped on the way to Venice. Some of this is just the pure unexpected pleasure of the menus' excess, illustrative beauty. We always love an overcharge of design, flair where none is necessary, since we register it emotionally as an overcharge of feeling—and we see this in the best menus.

When I look at the cover of the menu from the French pavilion to the 1939 World's Fair, for instance, I see past the menu to the fair itself. Though the war was a boom and boon to New York, where to European cities it was curse and catastrophe, this surely was the last time in history when the future looked so good, so charming. The double flags, hoisted high into the stratosphere on that menu cover are, in their streamlined mode, a tribute to the belle alliance of France and America, which had, too little remarked, lasted from 1870, and given us so much nice stuff: the statue in the harbor, early Hemingway, this menu. The muscular Ajax, the silhouetted figure who raises the double flags, red white and blue alike, of the two republics over the tiny little skyline of Manhattan below stands astride this entire, very blue globe, while the Eiffel Tower, demurely, waits across the ocean. All of a period's hope is caught in one image; and there is no nicer poster-notion of Franco-American amity—before the war and the fall of Paris and the bloody retaking, which left a state of suspicion where once there had been Paris and New York as the only features on the entire world, two cities alone on the big blue ball. Though New York would be richer after, it would never be so nice again. I imagine a couple—serener Fitzgeralds, lesser Murphys—who had been banished from the Left-Bank Babylon by the crash, absent from Paris since '29, eating and drinking here, the Closerie de Lilas recaptured in an afternoon in Queens. Every menu is, in this way, a kind of commercialized haiku; offering a mere compressed, laconic description of particular things, it opens windows to great sad vistas of memory. We see the dish, *Canard a l'orange,* and then our eyes scans right to the price—$3.95!—and a whole lost and enviable afternoon materializes for us. Was champagne ever so cheap as that? Was the duck flamed back then? Were they—and through them, we—ever so happy again? Menus are not merely forgotten promises, but hieroglyphic pleasures, kept forever in the open tomb of their achievement.

And then some of the pleasure of the scrutiny of a menu collection is that it opens not just windows looking out on lost loves, but whole doors to social history, particularly in this city. About that French pavilion alone, we know so much. We know that its chef, Henri Soule, stayed in the city, and so the French pavilion of the World's Fair became the Pavilion restaurant on Fifty-seventh Street, the first authentic three-star-style restaurant in the city. It in turn gave birth to a whole style, not at all Parisian really, of red banquettes, abundant flowers, small lamps on cozy tables, a style that soon included other restaurants, each with its own sweet menus: La Cote Basque, La Caravelle, Le Lavandou. The New York French restaurant (!) in all its ersatz glory—now nearly all gone save for La Grenouille and Le Perigord. So many flowers from that small seed.

Or we look at the menus of Luchows, once the primo place in the whole town, and we follow the traces of the city's story. We think of the way that the great restaurants once all clustered around 14th Street; how German preceded French as the primary language of good eating, how normal it once was to crowd into a summer beer garden. (You sometimes have the sense that nineteenth-century people, with their beer gardens and vast ice-skating rinks right in the middle of the park, used nature in the city far more festively than we do.) And the length of the Luchow's menu tells you something about the scale and ambition that were once thought necessary for a four-star, first-class place—and tells you something too about the arrangement of the old-style kitchen, where so much had to be made in advance and then just heated or prepped at the last moment for the diner.

So much *happens* in this town as we turn from menu to menu; good eating Frenchifies, then goes Italian; and then the Four Seasons opens (with the joke that it might have been the only way, in the endless gray of a New York autumn to winter to tell the four apart.) The Baum-Lang period begins, with its circus decors and preposterous names ("Forum of the Twelve Caesars" indeed!) with its saving, much-missed sense that dinner was first of all a form of fun, pure pleasure, before it was medicinal and ecologically sound—that dinner should be bright pink before it gets too green.

And yet for all those pleasures—worlds evoked, the city's story traced, and both done so simply through lists of dishes and titles and prices—there is still something more, some other pleasure harder to note. Perhaps it is simply that the theater of the restaurant has become so essential to our sense of ourselves that reading these menus is less like looking at old stage memorabilia and more like looking at the actual scripts of plays. We look at the menu and we see it all: the arrival under the awning, the coat-check girl under the stairs, the stroll to the table—is it good enough?—the linen napkin, the engagingly causal or haughtily remote waiter. (And we think: what stranger social institution could there be than the intimidating waiter, the kind Chaplin caught so perfectly in his films, the server turned to persecutor and snobbish condescender?)

And then, as our eye passes from entremets to entrées, we relive the small drama of choice, with its inevitable cognitive entanglement, its romantic extension:

"Oh, it all looks so delicious. . . . but, well, I was thinking of the lobster . . . ," she says tentatively, bright eyebrows over the menu's top edge, and you say, in the accents of the old mid-forties midtown, "Oh, spoil yourself! Let's have a lavish evening, price be dammed," and then four years later, you imagine yourself in the same place, same menu, and the small sane voice looks over the same choices (perhaps there is an additional dollar for the champagne, the *petits pois* are now $1.50 instead of $.75) and say, "Darling, you know the lobster doesn't always agree with *you*." To dessert or not to dessert; to dine or not to dine . . . New Yorkers loan out so much of their souls to the places that they eat at that the menu, the brief stenographic guides to those places, are imprinted, embossed, with the traces of our longings. Menus are the scenarios of happiness sought, the scripts of our small, bright plays of appetite, and when we open them at the Library, we once again become their actors.

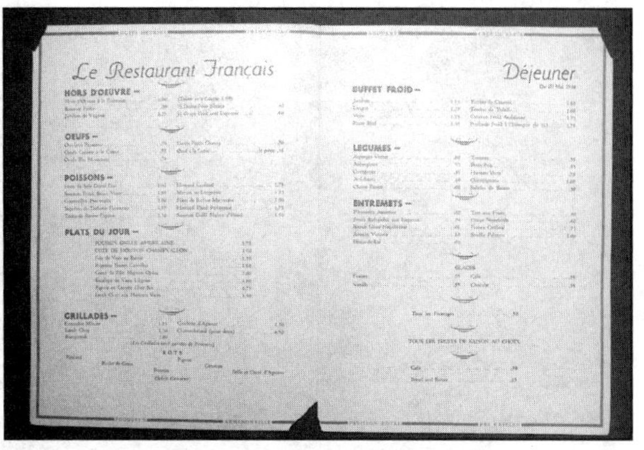

Le Restaurant Français

Déjeuner

HORS D'OEUVRE —

OEUFS —

POISSONS —

PLATS DU JOUR —

GRILLADES —

BUFFET FROID —

LEGUMES —

ENTREMETS —

ANNETTE GORDON-REED, professor of law and professor of history at Harvard University, and the Carole K. Pforzheimer Professor at the Radcliffe Institute for Advanced Studies at Harvard

ANNETTE GORDON-REED

Account Book, 1791–1803

Thomas Jefferson papers, 1765–1826

I chose to pose with one of the original volumes of Jefferson's memorandum books, his accounts of his daily expenditures, starting in 1767, when he was twenty-four years old, and ending in 1826, the year he died at age eighty-three. This volume covered the years 1791 to 1803, some of the most pivotal years of Jefferson's political life.

It's an invaluable record because he was so incredibly diligent about keeping it. He notes the date, his location, what he spent the money for, and how much. So not only are historians able to get some sense of his tastes, attitudes, and habits, we know where he is at all times. Most of the references are specific and understandable. Some are downright cryptic. One of my favorites is "The goose night." What?

I used the published version of the memorandum books extensively when writing *The Hemingses of Monticello*. I was stunned when I opened the Library's original copy to learn that Jefferson, in his very compulsive way, had created a name index. It does not appear in the published volumes. I turned to "H," and found Robert and James Hemings. They were Jefferson's wife's half-brothers, who began life in slavery and whom Jefferson freed in the 1790s. Their youngest sister was the famous Sally Hemings, Jefferson's longtime mistress. It was fascinating—and moving—to see them there listed under their family name.

PHILIP GOUREVITCH, writer and journalist

PHILIP GOUREVITCH

MELVILLE

"Bartleby, the Scrivener," Herman Melville

n.d. Gansevoort-Lansing collection, 1650–1919

It did not come easily to Melville—the great genius he bore. It came naturally, for sure. He was as alive with words and bursting with life and the world as any soul has ever been. But he had to work at it as well, his gift, and it took an incessant toll on him, not only because for too long his best work went unrecognized, but because of all that his intense perception of our human lot made him recognize. Vitality and gloom—the spark and the ember—are everywhere at once in his all-containing narratives. Because, yes, he contains us all as only the very greatest godlike wordsmiths do, that lonely company where Melville, the Manhattan seaman and customs clerk, sits between Shakespeare and Dylan. Melville was the first such master who was also an American, and he was the first American master whose society was the whole wide world. He seemed an ancient force, and he was impossibly modern—our literature has yet to catch up with the wild, free, tragic, and gleeful shape-shifting omnivorousness of his originality. Melville knew his elemental power. In the voice of Ishmael he told us what it felt like to write as he wrote: "Get me a condor's quill! Get me Vesuvius' crater for an inkwell! Friends, hold my arms!" Okay, he was sublime, but still he was a working man, which is what strikes one first on seeing this blue page, where with his quill and ink he jotted down an early and abandoned version of the penultimate moment of "Bartleby, the Scrivener"—the moment in which the narrator finds Bartleby dead in prison, and we readers understand somehow that something of us all died with him.

Melville subtitled Bartleby, "A Tale of Wall Street." It is that, and much more: Bartleby may seem a bit player cast aside from a Dickensian law chamber, but as Melville's brainchild he becomes a prototype for the next century's existentialist antiheroes, a dissident, a refusenik, the man who meets every task and temptation of quotidian life—and ultimately meets life itself—with the demurral, "I would prefer not to." For the narrator of this strange biography of this weird man—"one of those beings of whom nothing is ascertainable"—Melville gives us his almost complete opposite, an unquestioning bon vivant, who is drawn to Bartleby almost unconsciously, as to a mirror. In the most invisible figure in our midst, he finds the colossal image of all our kind, and in the last line of the story he tells us he knows it, when he signs off: "Ah, Bartleby! Ah, humanity!"

The published story is perfect, so what is gained by discovering in an acid-free box in the Library this ancient tossed-aside draft, in which only a few words of the finished story are the same, and the rest—those that were replaced in subsequent workings and reworkings, are all inferior in this version to the Melville we have lived with and loved? There is a small thrill, of course, in seeing the writer's hand on this old bit of paper, and in seeing how he worked. But the true astonishment is not this fragment of *Bartleby*, but what it shares the page with. Flip the paper upside down, and there, under the heading "Cards" is a list of the names of Melville's New York society—a mailing list of people to whom, presumably, he owed some correspondence. Dozens of names listed in two tiny columns. Did Melville make this list after giving up on this draft of *Bartleby*, or did he give up on the list to write his tale? Who knows? But there on the page is Bartleby's choice—between what is expected of one and the truth that can only be attained by refusing those expectations. Maybe Melville also mailed cards to his list, but he lives in us still because he knew what it meant to prefer not to.

> *Some few days after my last recorded visit, I again obtained admission to the Tombs and went through the yard in quest of Bartleby, but without finding him.*

"I saw him standing by the wall there some few hours ago," said a turnkey, maybe he's gone to his cell.

So saying he led the way a few steps, & pointed out the direction of the cell.

It was clean, well lighted & scrupulously whitewashed. The head-stone was standing up against the wall & stretched on a blanket at its base, his head touching the old marble, and his feet up the threshold lay the wasted form of Bartleby.

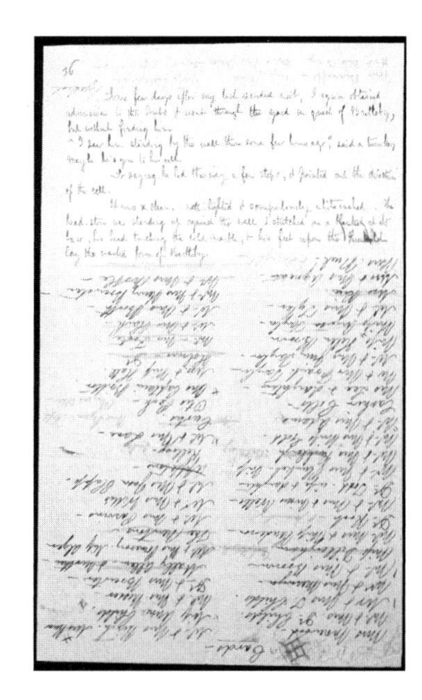

VARTAN GREGORIAN, president of the Carnegie Corporation of New York

VARTAN GREGORIAN

Declaration of Independence, July 4–10, 1776

Thomas Addis Emmet collection, 1483–1876

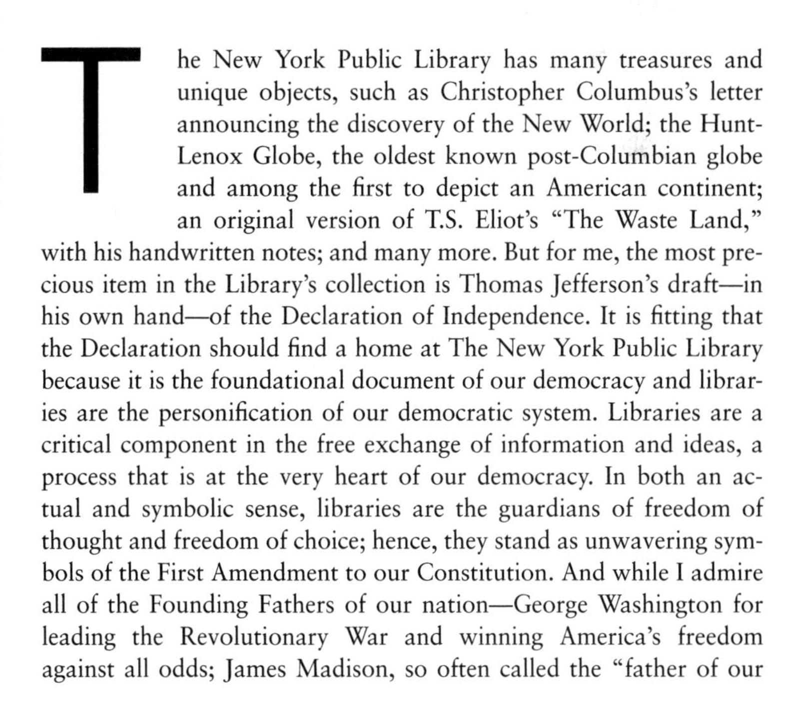

The New York Public Library has many treasures and unique objects, such as Christopher Columbus's letter announcing the discovery of the New World; the Hunt-Lenox Globe, the oldest known post-Columbian globe and among the first to depict an American continent; an original version of T.S. Eliot's "The Waste Land," with his handwritten notes; and many more. But for me, the most precious item in the Library's collection is Thomas Jefferson's draft—in his own hand—of the Declaration of Independence. It is fitting that the Declaration should find a home at The New York Public Library because it is the foundational document of our democracy and libraries are the personification of our democratic system. Libraries are a critical component in the free exchange of information and ideas, a process that is at the very heart of our democracy. In both an actual and symbolic sense, libraries are the guardians of freedom of thought and freedom of choice; hence, they stand as unwavering symbols of the First Amendment to our Constitution. And while I admire all of the Founding Fathers of our nation—George Washington for leading the Revolutionary War and winning America's freedom against all odds; James Madison, so often called the "father of our

Constitution"; and Benjamin Franklin, the consummate diplomat, statesman, inventor, and scientist—there is none I hold in higher esteem than Thomas Jefferson. This extraordinary man was the link between the European Age of Enlightenment and the light of democracy and freedom that he helped to bring forth in authoring the Declaration of Independence. It was Jefferson who articulated the principles that, even in our most trying hours, through hardship and conflict and challenge, both domestic and international, continue to provide strength to our nation. It was—and remains—Jefferson's vision that illuminates the path that leads the United States of America and its citizens into the future. Thomas Jefferson and democracy are eternally intertwined; so are libraries and democracy. That is why the irreplaceable Declaration of Independence is at the heart of the firmament of values that I rely on in my life and, I believe, define the life of our nation.

WORLD
BALL
HARLEM

THE HARLEM GLOBETROTTERS, basketball players

(previous pages)
THE HARLEM GLOBETROTTERS,
with globes from the Map Division.
(l to r in photo) Buckets Blakes,
Curly Neal, Big Easy Lofton.

THE HARLEM GLOBETROTTERS

Three globes from the Map Division

BLAKE HAZARD, musician

BLAKE HAZARD

William Blake,
Two Plates from *Europe a Prophecy*
Lambeth, 1794

I was very happy to discover that some of William Blake—my namesake's—loveliest etchings live in New York City, and thrilled to have a chance to visit them in the Library. As I held the centuries-old pages in my own hands, Blake's visions felt as fresh and strange as they must have in his own day. The gorgeous splashes of what look like freehand watercolors are bright and uninhibited. The lightly tattered edges seem to have been made so as much by his own energy as by the passing years.

As a musician, I'm struck by how relevant Blake's idiosyncratic process as an artist and a craftsman feel today. As a master of the written word and of the printmaking process (he created this loose, expressive relief style), he escaped the rigidity of the academy and of organized religion with his own sort of multimedia approach. These days artists are asked to communicate not just through their work but through social media, and to reveal their processes. Blake created his own text, his own medium, and was unafraid to speak about his passions. I find his fearlessness totally inspiring.

I think Blake, with all his love for the animal kingdom, would be glad to have his work protected by the fierce and pretty lions that guard the Public Library.

A.M. HOMES, writer, critic

A.M. HOMES

THE STUFF OF THE STUFF OF MAN

Jack Kerouac Realia

including Buddhist prayer bells, match books, lighter, spectacles, harmonica, playing cards, crayons, signal lantern, wooden crutches, and brown leather shoes

---

It is New York City, a moment fixed in time, there is the smoky scent of cigarettes, there are men playing chess, the sounds of the elevated subways, the feel of life lived underground, everything a little bit beat. And there is the music of conversation.

Jack Kerouac and his band of scribes were all about embracing and celebrating life, they were about talking and friendship and shooting the shit, having some drinks and getting laid and ruminating on the biggest question of all—existence. Compared to the average Joe they were wild—awe inspiring and threatening.

Working in spurts, Kerouac spewed "spontaneous bop prosody," or "jazz poetry." His writing was linguistic guerrilla warfare—a literary atom bomb, it smashed everything—it is everything and the kitchen sink—literally.

He gave writers permission to enter the world of flow—different from stream of consciousness; it was like being in the current, open to possibility, allowing creativity to move through the author, and the author to be one with both process and content. It was about embracing experience rather than resisting—it is the very roman candle Kerouac writes about in *On the Road*. His "spontaneous prose" is a kind of demolition derby pileup, a jazzy musical of words picking up speed and hurling themselves forward in a bumper car version of dialogue. Language and characters careen off each other, in a kind of doped deliciousness, the kind of down and dirty that never really washes off.

There is the romance of the track, the pungent smells of hay and horseshit and beer, the romance of the railroad, the greasy squeal of brakes. Rebirth and karma; Kerouac's peculiar and deeply personal combination of the workingman discussing astral bodies, karmic debt, past lives, and the selling of Jesus. It is about the power of ideas and the difficulty of escaping belief. And it is about the love of God and the fear of God—Kerouac, despite his interest, his exploration of Buddhism and Eastern philosophies, could never escape his Catholic upbringing.

What you see here object-wise is the stuff of man; the ephemera that which was kept in the pocket close to the bone—Jew's harp and harmonica, railroad watch and lantern, a red crayon and a yellow one, his shoes, his drivers license and library card, a corncob pipe and Zig- Zag rolling papers. These trinkets become artistic object lessons imbued with magic, they are lucky charm one meditates upon, the talisman that pushes us ever on.

SIRI HUSTVEDT, novelist, essayist, and poet

SIRI HUSTVEDT

Pen used by Charles Dickens

MICHAEL INMAN, Curator of Rare Books

MICHAEL INMAN

Leaves of Grass, Walt Whitman
1855
author's personal copy

If a first edition of *Leaves of Grass* is considered one of the holy grails of American literature, then the present volume is certainly the holiest of the holies. It is Whitman's personal copy of the book, into which the poet has sewn or pinned booklets containing his notes for future introductions and poems.

Leaves of Grass was, of course, a work in constant progress. Six distinct editions were published during Whitman's lifetime, each successively larger and more complex, eventually including nearly 400 poems. In contrast, the earliest edition was a much simpler affair—twelve untitled poems, occupying a mere ninety-five pages. Whitman printed 795 copies of this first version. Relatively few actually sold. Yet the lasting effect of this initial printing cannot be overstated. Even in its nascent form, the appearance of *Leaves of Grass* represented—along with contemporary works such as *Moby-Dick, Walden,* and Emerson's *Essays*—a significant moment in nineteenth-century letters: the first soundings of a truly American literary voice.

My relationship with Whitman (and I use that word, *relationship,* advisedly, as it seems that readers of *Leave of Grass* often develop a bond with the poet across the divide of time) began in middle school, in eighth-grade English class. Until that moment, what little poetry I had read seemed stilted and inaccessible. But here was something different. There was something in Whitman's style—in the plain-spoken language and rhythmic cadences; in the ebullient, celebratory nature of the writing; in the warmth and immediacy of his tone—that resonated with me. It was the first poetry I had encountered that felt familiar, with which I could relate.

Intrigued, I sought out more of his writing. By the time I reached graduate school, many years later, I had turned into a full-fledged Whitmaniac. I fondly recall countless hours spent in the university library stacks, researching not only the voluminous critical literature surrounding *Leaves of Grass* but also the work's textual and publication history. Over time this latter field of inquiry evolved into a general interest in publishing and the history of the book. A career in rare books librarianship loomed not far off. Nevertheless, had you told me that, one day, I would live in Whitman's beloved Manhattan, much less oversee The New York Public Library's renowned Oscar Lion Walt Whitman Collection, I likely would have laughed in disbelief. But such are the unexpected directions life takes you. Here I am.

Upon further reflection, it occurs to me that I owe a debt of gratitude to Whitman—after all, if only tangentially, he has been in the background of many of the interests and choices that have led me to where I am today. So thanks, Walt. It is good keeping company with you here at NYPL.

UZODINMA IWEALA, writer

UZODINMA IWEALA

To the Lighthouse, Virginia Woolf

holograph manuscript (3 v.) 1925–1927

I was supposed to read *To the Lighthouse* in college, but somehow managed to graduate with a degree in English literature never having done so. It wasn't until the year before I started medical school late one night at home in Nigeria that I picked up my fresh, unused paperback copy, started reading—"Yes, of course, if it's fine tomorrow . . ."—and never stopped.

The words of Virginia Woolf are so absorbing, her physical and mental landscapes enchanting. To say that she is one of the very best to have written in the English language is to parrot a legion of more learned individuals—some of whom grace the halls of The New York Public Library. I say so not to conform to consensus but because books like *To the Lighthouse* have drawn me deeper into literature as a whole, the playfulness of language, the rendering of sentiment, the importance of meaning, and the cataloging of experience, in short everything a library is supposed to house. It is fitting then that The New York Public Library houses the manuscript of *To the Lighthouse*, a fragile bound book with Woolf's actual penmanship—notes to self in the margin—etched in perfect lines across the page. What a thrill it is for someone like me, who writes in part because he likes the feel of fountain pen on paper and the look of words inked in lines across a page to be so close to the genesis of so great a literary work.

The written word is permanent once it occupies space on the page, but permanent does not mean static or lifeless. Whether on the fragile pages of an eighty-year-old notebook or the fresh leaves of a unused college bookstore paperback, Woolf lives and inspires the smartest scholars who have spent years studying her and those who stumble across her alike. How important it is that we have right here, in this city, an institution that can cater to both.

To the Library then!

BILL T. JONES, cofounder and artistic director of Bill T. Jones / Arnie Zane Dance Company

BILL T. JONES

"San Francisco Bay Blues," Jesse Fuller

n.d., from *The Great Blues Men,* Vanguard: 1972

One-man band Jesse Fuller, whose nickname was "Lone Cat," was born in Georgia in 1896. It wasn't until he was in his fifties that he thought of making a professional life from music. Before that he'd shined shoes and worked in a broom factory and in a quarry, among many other itinerate jobs. He'd cut his teeth playing blues, ballads, spirituals, and instrumentals but had only earned money from music by passing a hat.

Finally, in the 1950s he got the idea to play music professionally. He tried to start a band but found other musicians too unreliable, so he set himself up as a one-man show, playing the twelve-string guitar, harmonica, kazoo, washboard, cymbal, and even an instrument he dreamed up one night in bed, called the fotdella. The fotdella is a six-string bass, played with an equal number of foot pedals directing felt hammers against the strings, a bit like a piano.

When I came to the Library, I wanted to choose something that had a profound resonance with me. "San Francisco Bay Blues" really put Jesse Fuller on the map, but the song that I felt perhaps even more deeply connected to was "Everybody Works but Father." I was twenty-two when I was invited to come perform in Central Park at the

New York Shakespeare Festival, which was—and still is—a very big deal. It was unusual for a young dancer/choreographer to have chosen to perform a piece by Jesse Fuller—the words of which were "Everybody works at my house but my old man."

A lot of my work at that time was poking at painful scabs. Jesse Fuller's music sounded like "darkie music." "Everybody Works but Father" was a piece about people, and about unemployment, and when I think about this piece, I see how I was imperfectly, and in a very naive way, exploring ideas of place, time, and identity long before people were doing "identity work."

The stage piece started out with a sound reminiscent of Native American chanting—which had been devised by Arnie Zane and me at the bedside of Linda Berry as she was recovering from a terrible car accident we'd all been in together. We got through her recuperation sitting beside her with a tape recorder and singing. I was on a pair of homemade block shoes dressed in black trousers, a white shirt, and tie. I thought that I looked like Malcolm X, but others said I looked like a windmill.

I spoke my social security number over and over, and while I was doing it, I was stripping down to a pair of green boxer shorts. It ended with me spinning in Central Park shouting, "I love you."

One critic noted that I was a humanist and that she didn't know if anyone else would do what I did, that I was worth watching, and yet when I think back to that performance, it was all very low-tech. I wasn't a svelte technician, but the piece struck me and struck audiences. I had something that was charming and winning, I was just young, affable, and extremely ambitious, an extroverted young dude who had his moment on the stage and was doing it with real sincerity and a bit of a lark.

Perhaps I was so drawn to Jesse Fuller because his music gave me a glimpse into my parents' time and I was looking for clues to their lives, or maybe it struck me as an Americana that I couldn't possibly know.

SHARON JONES, singer

SHARON JONES

Eight Bells, Winslow Homer

etching, 1887, Print Collection, Miriam and Ira D. Wallach Division of Art, Prints and Photographs

The perfect break from the wear of the road is fishing. There's nothing like grabbing my gear, heading out of the craziness of the city, and finding a quiet pond for some "Sharon Time." Check out my song "Fish in the Dish" off of *Naturally.* That's where me and the boys tell it like it is—ain't no time for messin' when it comes to fishing.

When I got to The New York Public Library I was floored by the prevailing Pisces inspiration that filled the room—paintings and books full of fish; all different species of fish . . . even my dress looked like it had fish scales on it.

This all reminded me of a story about one of my fishing trips. I was still really young, so I didn't have all my gear yet—just a hook and a reel, not even any bait! So I cast my line out and pretty soon I feel a tug. "I caught something!" Meanwhile, all these other kids were making fun of me, "Sharon, you just got a branch!" I showed them—I pulled out a huge bass fish. This boy comes up and he wanted to help me cut the fish off my line . . . and I'm looking at him, thinking I don't know if he knows what he's doing . . . So he's cutting the line and *he drops my fish in the water* and I see my fish go swimming away! So I pick up his bike and throw it in too. Don't mess with my fishing!

MICHAEL KIMMELMAN, author, art critic, and columnist for *The New York Times*

MICHAEL KIMMELMAN

RAY JOHNSON AT THE LIBRARY

A skwlaene boolk, Ray Johnson

collaged artist's book, ca. 1955, Spencer Collection

The slender exhibition catalog, now more than half a century old, is something of a mystery, as is the artist who tinkered with it. David Christie, a specialist in prints at the Library, retrieved the booklet from the Spencer Collection without, he admitted, knowing much about it. He knew only that it had come into the Library's possession during the mid-1990s, acquired as part of a stash of so-called mail art.

The object? A paperback catalog for a Paul Klee show at the Curt Valentin Gallery, from 1953. Valentin, the great German-born dealer, having fled Hitler for New York in 1937, shepherded the works of many leading European modernists into the city. This show was one of his last. He died in 1954.

And the artist? Not Klee, precisely. Ray Johnson. He of the "mail art." Johnson, largely unknown in his lifetime, has achieved a measure of posthumous fame since his suicide in 1995, at sixty-seven, and partly because of it too. He was a pioneer of Conceptualism and Pop, a mandarin of collage, wordplay, and mischief, cultivated, via legendary Black Mountain College, in the circle of John Cage and Robert Rauschenberg. Among other things, Johnson devised inscrutable, coded collages that he photocopied and distributed through the United States Postal Service to countless, frequently unsuspecting recipients, who as often as not simply tossed these gifts into the garbage, which was fine by Johnson. It was the gesture and exchange, or lack thereof, that counted. He also organized "nothings," his version of 1960s "happenings," although his dealer, Frances Beatty, once admitted she could never be quite sure whether by "doing nothing" Johnson meant he would do a nothing, or do a gallery show that had nothing in it, or that he was simply doing nothing.

In any case, the Klee catalog is a classic of Johnsonian collage. He mixed with the booklet's printed text and images clippings from magazines and newspapers, including a few panels from a 1954 *Brenda Starr* comic strip. On the cover, interspersed with the four letters in the name KLEE he wrote ASWANBK, adding, between the B and K, part of a newspaper advertisement for a swimming pool showing a diver beside the letters OOL (cut out from the word POOL). Deciphered, this becomes, more or less, "A Klee Swan Book." Johnson loved puns and anagrams. Inside he added images of swans and also ducks, including a rubber duck from a soap advertisement showing a smiling toddler in a bathtub alongside the words "NEW Johnson's BABY." Johnson, as self-regarding as the next artist, loved dumb jokes, too.

Presuming 1954, or thereabouts, is the date Johnson tinkered with this catalog, we are talking about one of the early examples of Pop Art. It was typical that Johnson would help usher in one of the past century's most storied movements in such an easily overlooked fashion—typical of the Library too that it should yield up such a gem from the archives. A minor gem of visual irony, cunningly drawn in ways that play duet with Klee's pictures, Johnson's work adds a kind of Whitman-like whimsy and cool to the older master's Swiss refinement.

I suspect Johnson, who craved fame while contriving to shun it (the paradox of his spectacular suicide), would have loved his work ending up in the Library, waiting to be discovered like all the odds and ends he scavenged from the street or cut out of old magazines and made into art. Combining far flung texts with images, his life's work was all about seeing what miracles sprang up from that cocktail. It was akin to the Library's mission in that obvious sense, as was the refusal of his art to be pigeonholed, its democracy and its celebration of the messy eloquence and complexity of the city.

KAKI KING, guitarist and composer

KAKI KING

Insurance Maps of Atlanta, Georgia

Sanborn Map Company, 1931–1932

aps, both geographical and political, have always fascinated me. One can look at an ancient illuminated navigational map, complete with drawings of sea monsters and insets of the heavenly spheres, and marvel at the medieval mind that so delicately put on paper the collected knowledge of the world's coastlines. Contemporary political maps with each country bursting in a single color make modern cartographers seem like children armed with a coloring book and bright crayons.

Humankind has been both guided and beguiled by the maps it creates. These daubs of pastel and dotted lines have held the human stories of discovery, of movement, of triumph and vanquishment. If all that were left of earthly civilization were a stack of maps and charts, I would imagine that a fairly accurate summary of human history could be recreated. A history, for better or worse, written by the victors.

During my recent visit to the Map Division at The New York Public Library I was able to view maps of my own family history. A Reconstruction-era map of Georgia showed me that the tiny towns my family hails from were not just extant but thriving in the late 1800s. Another map showed an early grid of the city of Atlanta, decades before the concept of urban sprawl had entered American consciousness. My absolute favorite was the very detailed map of the city block where my parents' law firm is now located, circa 1950. The building, now affectionately known as "The King Building," was highlighted in pink.

I was truly mesmerized by the few maps that I saw, trailing my finger across the counties and towns like a child, my mouth agape. The most wonderful thing about this is that anyone can come to the Library and request such materials. Ever wonder what the subdivision you were born in looked like a hundred years ago? Go ask the Library to help you find out.

Of course, the greatest maps of all are the geographic ones. Here a green mountain range, here an endless forest, here a shallow river crossing a desert, and none of the arbitrary splotches of color and dotted lines that humans fight over endlessly. Then again, maybe maps have been the key ingredient in the creation of modern culture. The idea that an ephemeral imaginary line can create a national identity is both comical and yet deadly serious. Hopefully these identities will in turn create better ideas about how to treat the planet and the people on it. That is a tale to be told by the victors.

NICK LAIRD, novelist and poet

NICK LAIRD

"The Wild Swans at Coole," William Butler Yeats
holograph manuscript, unsigned, 1917

THOMAS G. LANNON, assistant curator, Manuscripts and Archives Division

THOMAS G. LANNON

Sumerian Tablets, ca. 2450–1600 B.C.E.

In his 1961 *Guide to Archives and Manuscripts in the United States,* Philip Hamer introduced the Manuscripts and Archives Division at NYPL as including "9,000,000 pieces comprising adequate to superb examples of the recorded word, in most of its media, periods, and tongues." This helps to explain the collection of Sumerian tablets, dating from circa 2450 to 1600 B.C.E., held in the Library as examples of cuneiform script.

Cuneiform writing emerged from the practice of marking clay to record transactions in economy and property. Applied to characters of ancient inscriptions from Persia and Assyria, the term *cuneiform* was invented by antiquarians of the eighteenth century. From Latin *cuneus,* meaning "wedge," cuneiform script is simply one composed with wedges. As science changed in the wake of the Newtonian advance, *sola scriptura* gave way to historicist criticism. Francis Bacon's structure of knowledge aligned functions of mind with correlated subjects. The function of memory lined up next to history. Bacon's inductive method involved the observation and compilation of phenomena for which history turned to antiquities, or literally *physical remainders.* Philological study of texts as physical remainders would flourish into the nineteenth century. With the help of positivism and theories of evolution, the date of Creation was slowly pushed back to include centuries before the book of Genesis. Expeditions to the lands around the Tigris and Euphrates rivers yielded more physical remainders, each offering a glimpse of the civilization's so-called cradle.

In 1855, Nelson Eames and his wife, Harriet Pheobe (Crane) Eames, moved to Brooklyn, New York, with their six-year-old son, Wilberforce. The boy did not attend high school and was by his fifteenth year working as a "printer's devil" at a local newspaper, the *East New York Sentinal.* Devoted to print, Eames eventually found work as a clerk in Brooklyn book shops. At the age of thirty, Eames landed the plum job of personal assistant to Dr. George Henry Moore, the head of the Lenox Library in Manhattan. Upon Dr. Moore's death, Eames became assistant librarian and later librarian. Employment at the Lenox Library ensured a life in close contact to the printed word. He would spend his days next to editions of the *Bay Psalm Book,* Milton, the *Geography* of Ptolemy, and voyages of Captain John Smith and Sir Walter Raleigh. Incidentally, he would spend his nights on top of books. Eames's obituary includes a description of his home so thoroughly crammed with books that a swinging hammock was the only way to move about. Eames never left the United States, but through books had knowledge of Chinese, Japanese, and Bantu dialects of Africa. Without traveling, Eames collected some seven to eight hundred clay tablets, cones, and seals from ancient Sumeria. Along with ten volumes of his acquisition records for these objects, they eventually became part of the collection of The New York Public Library.

And so I hold this piece of clay marked with a series of wedges. The tablets are a kind of administrative record. Research has proven them to list agricultural activities, animals in the care of a person, expenditures for services such as a day's work or basket made, and wages received and owed. Without repeating and with only so many known in existence, each is terribly rare and uniquely individual. Within a group, each tablet is an only known copy. As unique impressions of symbols, the meaning of which are possibly lost to time, Eames's Babylonian collection is reminder of the purpose of a manuscript collection in a research library.

IMAM KHALID LATIF, executive director and chaplain (imam) of The Islamic Center at New York University

IMAM KHALID LATIF

Declaration of Independence

July 4, 1776

Two hundred and thirty-five years have passed since the Declaration of Independence was written. In many of those years, including the most recent that has passed, groups and individuals from around the world have stood up for their rights just as our Founding Fathers did on that fateful day. It is easy to draw inspiration from their example as they gathered from across thirteen individual colonies to unite as states and to collectively decide that they as leaders would no longer let their people be treated unjustly, that no individual, be they king or tyrant, has the right to infringe upon anyone's relationship with God, and integral to that relationship are rights of equality, democracy, and self-determination.

I am not sure how many Muslims have ever held an original copy of the Declaration of Independence in their hands. I would venture not many. One can safely assume that some would be shocked at the idea that such a thing could even happen. Many people believe Islam has no place in the United States, that all Muslims should be viewed through a lens of suspicion, and that maybe we should just go back home. I am home, though. I was born here, I was raised here, and I wouldn't want to be anywhere else.

Muslims have been a part of the American narrative even before our country's independence, with the first Muslims coming to the New World as African slaves throughout the slave trade. Our legacy has been rich and deep since that time, and today close to 6 million Muslims from all the world live in the United States, 800,000 of which call New York their home. We are by no means a homogeneous community but rather are as diverse as the very country we live in. It is hard to justifiably stereotype us, as really the only thing that all Muslims are is different from one another, like most human beings. We do share some things in common, though, with our brothers and sisters in humanity. Indeed we as men are created equal and each of us respectively has been endowed with certain God-given rights, as our Founding Fathers cemented forever in their Declaration of Independence for generations of Americans to come. I have the right to live, I have the right to be free, and I have the right to seek out happiness in hopes of finding contentment. And so should everyone else.

FRAN LEBOWITZ, writer

FRAN LEBOWITZ

Nancy Drew Novels by Carolyn Keene

Question: Why did you choose Nancy Drew?

Answer: I chose Nancy Drew because the letter I received asked me to choose something from the collections that "spoke to me very personally," and since I associate books that affected me very personally with childhood, and since, although I would have liked to have been the sort of child who was affected very personally by the Gutenberg Bible or Holle's 1482 printing of Ptolemy's *Cosmographia,* I was, in fact, not. So it wasn't until I came across a listing under the somewhat sad heading "As Well As," and I saw the Stratemeyer Syndicate, publishers of the Hardy Boys, the Bobbsey Twins, and Nancy Drew—including all the original artwork—that my heart leapt.

One of the things the Nancy Drew books can do, which really all books could do to me when I was a child, was that they could completely take you. You would become wholly absorbed in them. And I still require that from books. I think a book is bad if I'm aware when I'm reading that I'm reading. That is a minimum requirement for a book. So I believe that the Nancy Drew books set a high and enduring standard.

Being a girl in the 1950s and 1960s was nothing like being a girl now. So I suppose the idea of a girl detective, an autonomous figure—because she didn't have a mother, and her father was very indulgent and hardly ever there, and she had a housekeeper and most importantly, a roadster, and she could just do whatever she wanted—this was incredibly attractive to me. And I think to all girls of my age. Because being a child in the United States in the 1950s and 1960s was kind of like living in Communist Russia. There was universal surveillance of children then. So the freedom aspect was tremendously appealing.

But when I was my early forties, I was told by an Episcopalian priest—hence, I was forced to believe her—that she had written a Nancy Drew book. And she explained to me about this Stratemeyer Syndicate. I was devastated. In fact, I still have not recovered. I believed in Carolyn Keene. I believed there was such a person. I believed in Laura Lee Hope, who wrote the Bobbsey Twins books. I believed these were real people. Finding out that there was no Carolyn Keene in my early forties was probably similar to the experience that gentiles have upon discovering there is no Santa Claus, which also seems to occur in their early forties. This was the only thing I believed in, and I was crushed. So I think that *syndicate* is exactly the right word.

STAFF OF THE LIBRARY FOR THE PERFORMING ARTS, (l to r): Jonathan Hiam, curator, American Music Collection and the Rodgers and Hammerstein Archives of Recorded Sound; George Boziwick, chief, Music Research Division; Robert Kosovsky, curator, Rare Books and Manuscripts, Music Research Division; Karen Burke, assistant chief, Music Research Division

LIBRARY FOR THE PERFORMING ARTS MUSIC DIVISION STAFF

Arnold Schoenberg Portrait, Man Ray

1927

The Library's 1927 portrait of Arnold Schoenberg by Man Ray represents a lineage of twentieth-century American composition that sits at the very center of the Music Division's archival collections, a lineage which includes the pioneering works of Henry Cowell and the great musical experiments of John Cage. The deep connections between these three composers betray the pronounced individuality of each artist's music, yet the personal and professional interactions among them arguably defined the direction American music would take during the second half of the twentieth century.

In the early 1930s, John Cage found a mentor in Henry Cowell, first in California and later in New York City. Cowell, whose deep interest in the music of non-Western cultures informed his experiments in expanding the palette of admissible musical sounds, created new pathways for the next generation of composers to explore. As such, his position at the epicenter of experimental music in the United States, both as a composer and as the publisher of the influential *New Music Quarterly*, led Cage to dub Cowell the "open sesame for new music in America." Thus when Cowell suggested that Cage study with the renowned Austrian, Arnold Schoenberg, a recent émigré to Los Angeles, Cage followed Cowell's advice. In preparation, Cage began studying in New York with composer Adolph Weiss, an unheralded advocate for new music, a close friend of Cowell, and the first American to have studied with Schoenberg. Cage's subsequent time with Schoenberg proved formative, even if their musical philosophies differed widely, and he would go on to cite Schoenberg as one of the most important influences in his life as a composer.

The Music Division is home to both the papers of Henry Cowell and the manuscript scores of John Cage. As such, we play our part in fostering the legacy of two foundational figures in the history of American music. We strive to demonstrate the connections among our vast collections, and for this reason the Schoenberg portrait is exemplary. Inscribed in the lower right-hand corner, Schoenberg commended the photo "to my dear friend, Adolph Weiss, cordially wishing that to him, I might always look better than I am (as this picture is better than its model)." In this way, the portrait closes a circle, one which helped define an important strain of music history and one which we are humbled to care for in our role at The New York Public Library for the Performing Arts.

—Jonathan Hiam, curator

MAYA LIN, artist and architect

MAYA LIN

CONCERNING ATKINS

Photographs of British Algae, Anna Atkins
cyanotype impressions, 1843–1853, Spencer Collection

I have long been an admirer of Anna Atkins's work—partially because it presents one of the most ethereal images of nature and partially because the printing technique, the cyanotype, holds the same syntax as the blueprint, a method that any architect would be familiar with. Atkins's seemingly mundane subject matter and printing technique were so transformed through her artistic lens, it became something ghostly and otherworldly. By placing the plants directly on the photographic paper and exposing the pages to sunlight, she was able to create real-scale silhouettes. These contact prints seem to float upon the page and are some of the most beautiful images I have ever seen of the natural world.

Like Atkins, many of my artworks are derived from looking at the natural world—but with a technological bent. My art sees the world through a twenty-first-century lens, using modern-day technologies, such as sonar mappings of the ocean floor, satellite views of the earth, and topographic studies of the natural terrain, which allow me to reveal aspects of the world that we may not necessarily be paying attention to. The idea of examining and interpreting natural forms are what draws me to Atkins's works.

I first came across Atkins at the Getty Museum, and was so pleased to find them in The New York Public Library's collections.

Nothing can compare to being able to actually see and experience these works firsthand. The beauty and tactility of the printed form, even, or perhaps especially, as it ages, is something that I so value in these incredible works on paper.

MAIRA LIRIANO, manager, The Irma and Paul Milstein Division of United States History, Local History and Genealogy

MAIRA LIRIANO

New York Panorama: A Comprehensive View of the Metropolis

by the Federal Writers' Project, 1938, and other WPA pieces

The New York Public Library is described as "education without tuition" in the delightful book *New York Panorama: A Comprehensive View of the Metropolis* by the Federal Writers' Project, published in 1938. This book and the *New York City Guide: A Comprehensive Guide to the Five Boroughs of the Metropolis: Manhattan, Brooklyn, the Bronx, Queens, and Richmond,* published the following year, were two major works produced during the Great Depression by a program of the Works Progress Administration (WPA). The WPA, established by Franklin D. Roosevelt, in 1935 employed millions of people to do public works. At its peak, the WPA employed 250,000 people in New York City. Two soon-to-be famous writers, John Cheever and Richard Wright, were among those employed, and they contributed to the fantastic descriptions and historical details found in these guidebooks.

The WPA also employed 400 relief workers, mostly women, to work at the Library. They set up an open-air library in Bryant Park, prepared bibliographies, and produced another of my favorite things in the Division, the *New York City Scrapbooks.* These fifty-six volumes of image clippings and original photographs, arranged primarily by street, were the precursors to image searches on the Web.

I have always been fascinated by the works of the WPA and was intrigued to discover that some of that work lives on at the Library. We still use the scrapbooks and guidebooks, and you can view the beautiful murals by Edward Laning on the third floor.

JOHN LITHGOW, actor, musician, and author

JOHN LITHGOW

WHAT IT WAS LIKE

Central Park

published by John Bachmann

1863

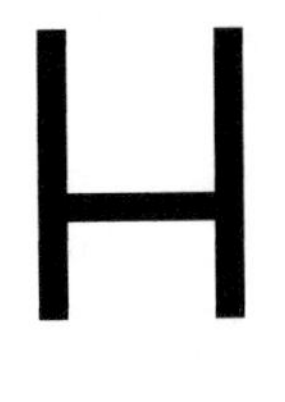

ow did they know? A hundred and sixty years ago, when the area from 59th Street to 125th Street was nothing but woods and farmland, New York's prescient city fathers foresaw the absolute necessity of Central Park. They engaged surveyors to stride through the open fields of the middle island and to plot the grid of a Manhattan-to-be. In their wisdom, they reserved hundreds of acres in the geographic center to provide the expanding city with its heart and its lungs. Sure enough, in the coming years the metropolis grew up around this elegant sylvan rectangle. Central Park lies there today between the Upper East and West sides like a pampered courtesan. No citizen of Manhattan can imagine the city without it.

I've lived in New York off and on for forty years. Every home I've ever had in the city was on the Upper West Side. A life of striving has allowed me to realize a long-held dream: for the last few years I've lived in one of the great old Central Park West buildings within yelling distance of The Natural History Museum. Central Park at long last has become my front yard. In my eyes, there is no better place to live, anywhere. So a few months ago, with the zeal of an *arriviste,* I went down to The New York Public Library's stately Stephen A. Schwarzman Building with a modest request. I asked the Library staff to give me a little glimpse into the history of my new neighborhood and of the vast parkland just across the street from it.

Needless to say, the Stephen A. Schwarzman Building has a pretty splendid history of its own. When librarian Matt Knutzen led me into the Map Division, he might as well have been escorting me into the nineteenth century. Dark wood and richly bound books surrounded us, with a marble floor underfoot and an ornate ceiling overhead. On broad wooden tables, Mr. Knutzen had arranged a series of plats, maps, and drawings, each as large as a theater poster in Shubert Alley. The documents showed their century-old age but they were in mint condition. They were arranged chronologically, starting in the year 1776, with intervals of ten or twenty years separating them. As we proceeded from one document to another, I saw the vast tract of Central Park and its urban environs evolve before my eyes.

There were maps showing villages, farms, and estates, long since forgotten. There were Frederick Law Olmsted's preliminary sketches laying out the park's plazas, allées, and bridal paths. There were surveyor's plans plotting the nearby streets and avenues, decades before anyone dreamed that automobiles would drive down them or that subways would roar by below. There was graphic evidence of power plants, railroad tracks, elevated trams, and Hudson River docks in locations where there are now not the slightest traces of them. Each document seemed to shimmer with a radioactive mixture of familiarity and unfamiliarity. The Manhattan on display on those tables belonged simultaneously to us present-day citizens of the city and to a huge population of shadowy New Yorkers from a century and a half in the past.

I had asked, "What did my neighborhood look like when it first turned into a city?" Mr. Knutzen had obliged me, seemingly without effort. He had marshaled the exhaustive resources of his mighty institution, overwhelming me with information, documentation, and vivid images. As I staggered out of the Map Division, drunk with new knowledge, a dizzying thought crossed my mind. I could have asked a million such questions and The New York Public Library would have handily answered them all.

LARISSA MACFARQUHAR, staff writer at *The New Yorker*

LARISSA MACFARQUHAR

HENRY JAMES

"Coquelin," Henry James
holograph manuscript
Sept. 18, 1886

I don't like precious books. First editions, inscribed copies, fragile, crumbling leather things—there's something so *precious* about them. I prefer paperbacks to hardbacks, and I'd rather read a battered book that I can bend and write in than a beautifully bound edition I must treat with reverence.

There is something fascinating about the smell and feel of old books, but that's the smell and feel of pastness per se, nothing particularly bookish about it. So entering the sanctum of the Library's Berg Collection and sitting down in front of the manuscript of Henry James's 1887 essay for *The Century,* "Coquelin," which I was permitted only barely to touch, not to pick up, never to take out of the room, I felt I was there under false pretenses. What could be so thrilling about a manuscript? Why lay these scribbled pages on green felt and, afterward, replace them in some carefully climate-controlled book vault? The writing process is interesting, sure, but why make relics of its debris? I looked at the manuscript. I bent closer. I could read—nothing. James's handwriting was graceful, tidy, evenly paced, and incomprehensible. With effort, I began to make out words, but the lines, the shapes, the gestures, and the pen that made them were from a society so removed from mine that even once I became used to them there could be no fluency in the reading. It was annoying. But that, of course, I realized, was the value of the thing. It's so easy to read anything in type that you can fancy yourself fully inside the mind and time that produced it. Which is part of the pleasure of reading. But to move away from that false lingua franca, to move backward into handwriting, is to be forced to know how deeply foreign and opaque other minds and times really are.

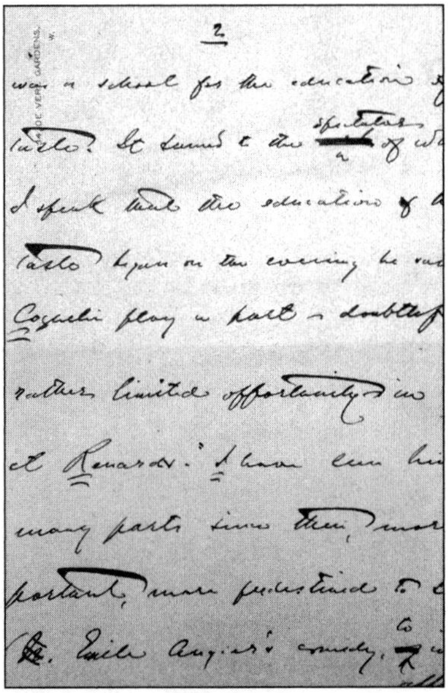

DE VERE GARDENS, W.

2

was a school for the education of

taste. It seemed to the spectators of which

I speak that the education of

taste began on the evening he saw

Coquelin play a part — doubtless

rather limited opportunity in

et Renard'. I have seen him

many parts since then, more

portant, more predestined to

. Emile Augier's comedy, to

STAFF OF THE LIONEL PINCUS AND PRINCESS FIRYAL MAP DIVISION (l to r): Katherine Cordes, manager; Matthew Knutzen, geospatial librarian

MAP DIVISION

Grooten atlas, oft Werelt beschryving...,
Joan Blaeu
copper plate engraving, colored by hand
1648–1664

ZARELA MARTINEZ, restaurateur

ZARELA MARTINEZ

"Watergate: pero de que escandalo me hablan?"
Pablo Neruda, typescript article for *The New York Times*
1973

ULYSSES

COLUM McCANN, novelist

(previous pages)
COLUM McCANN with *Ulysses*

COLUM McCANN

INELUCTABLE MODALITY OF THE VISIBLE

Ulysses, James Joyce

Paris: Shakespeare & Co., 1922

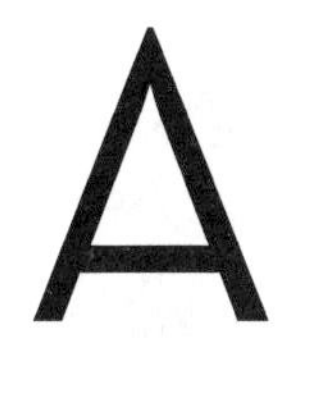

simple part of the charm of books is that they disintegrate. No book can be protected forever. There are simple laws of nature, maybe even laws of God. Even if we sealed our books in hermetic tombs, some distant day entropy will gnaw at the pages. It's called age—it's the most democratic thing in the world and it happens to the best of us, even James Joyce.

So now a confession: There is a beautiful copy of *Ulysses* in The New York Public Library's Stephen A. Schwarzman Buliding. A first edition. Signed by Joyce to his friend James Stephens. The collision of book and place is, for me, sacred. I adore the Library: it's the finest in the world. And I love the book: it's the greatest novel ever written. So when I had a chance to see the copy of *Ulysses* down on 42nd Street and Fifth Avenue, I let my tired heart hammer away. Into the Library. Up the stairs. Into the Berg Collection reading room. The book was opened carefully and methodically, and I was supervised every moment of the way. I didn't even get to touch the pages. I leaned over them, breathed them in. *The ineluctable modality of the visible.* But when the book was put away a tiny flake of page fell from inside onto the blue cloth beneath. This happens. Books will flake. A crumb, really. The book was put away. Wrapped, protected, humified. But the miniscule flake still lay there. It would soon become dust. I stared at it. And then I did what any heartsick lovesick booksick wordsick worldsick joycesick fool would do.

I ate it.

There have been other times in my life when *Ulysses* has entered my body. This is the beauty of books. They arrive inside us in the most peculiar ways. The messy layers of human experience get ordered and reordered by what we take into our minds. Books can carry us to the furthest side of our desires. We can travel, we can remain, we can hide in plain sight. We can hoist our history into a page. We too will die and disintegrate, but the amazing thing is that the stories don't die with us. Death takes away everything, except what we need to tell others. This too then is the beauty of libraries. They allow us this manner of living. Libraries are, in a very pure sense, places where we can learn to remain alive.

Perhaps I should apologise to all at the Library for touching my finger against that tiny flake of *Ulysses,* then putting it on my tongue in the manner of a man who has known other churches. But the fact is the blue cloth would have been collected, and then someone would have shaken it out, and the tiny flake would have been swept away, and it would have been gone. Ashes don't return to wood. Words, on the other hand, stay with us. Yes, they do, indeed. Yes.

PATRICK McGRATH, novelist and short-story writer

PATRICK McGRATH

Sketches for "Archduke Trio," Op.97, Ludwig van Beethoven

1810 or 1811

Inventions, Johann Sebastian Bach

manuscript, ca. 1750

I first saw this manuscript in the early 1980s while writing captions for an exhibition of various of the Library's treasures. It was coupled with a score handwritten by Johann Sebastian Bach. Bach's notation was flawless. It seemed a perfect expression of those eighteenth-century ideals of sanity, clarity, and proportion.

Beethoven's hand belongs to a different order of musician altogether. Here's the sort of artist Diderot may have been thinking of when he wrote: "It is then that genius takes his lamp and lights it. And this dark, solitary, savage bird, this untamable creature, with his gloomy melancholy plumage, opens his throat and begins his song, makes the groves resound and breaks the silence and the darkness of the night."

In Beethoven's manuscript we glimpse in embryo two movements of the "Archduke" Trio, the *Scherzo* and the *Andante cantabile.* The sketches were made in 1810, the work completed a year later, and performed for the first time in public in April 1814. Beethoven was himself the pianist that night, but the performance was a bitter disappointment. His *forte* was crashingly loud, his *piano* in places inaudible. Apparently he didn't know that the instrument he was playing was out of tune. Many of those present were moved to tears by these tragic indications of the composer's worsening deafness. He never performed in public again. Despite his deafness, however, he went on to compose numerous works unequalled in the canon of classical music.

The archduke to whom the trio is dedicated was Rudolph, younger brother of the Emperor of Austria, an epileptic and sickly man, but in his own right a distinguished pianist and composer. With the help of two other aristocrats the archduke secured Beethoven's lifelong financial security. Beethoven devoted more than a dozen works to him.

Beethoven died in 1837, four years before his great patron. The archduke is buried in the Imperial Crypt in Vienna, although his heart is elsewhere, in the crypt of St. Wenceslas Cathedral in Olomouc, in the present-day Czech Republic.

Beethoven fulfilled the destiny that seems ordained for him in this wildly scribbled and overwritten manuscript. He died in a thunderstorm, and at the moment of his death a peal of thunder was heard. An autopsy revealed significant liver damage. He is buried in the Wahring Cemetery, northwest of Vienna.

When I first saw his manuscript next to Bach's, I thought I'd chanced upon a revealing instance of cultural tension: Baroque propriety and Romantic vigor in stark opposing contrast, the character of each made plain in the handwriting of a great composer.

But no. The Bach is a fair copy of a finished score. The Beethoven is just a pair of preliminary sketches. But they are in his hand, and for this reason to be treasured.

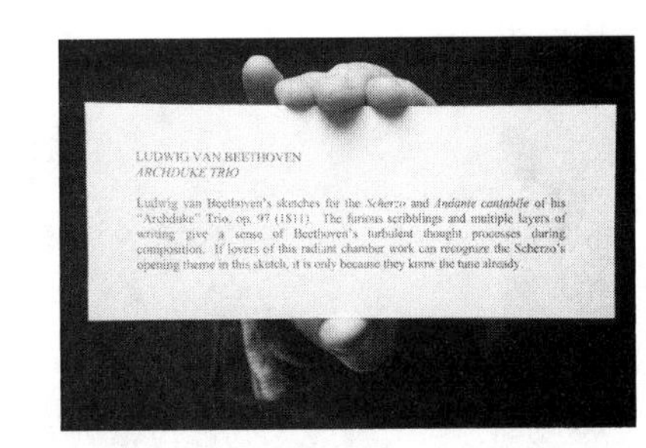
LUDWIG VAN BEETHOVEN
ARCHDUKE TRIO
Ludwig van Beethoven's sketches for the Scherzo and Andante cantabile of his "Archduke" Trio, op. 97 (1811). The furious scribblings and multiple layers of writing give a sense of Beethoven's turbulent thought processes during composition. If lovers of this radiant chamber work can recognize the Scherzo's opening theme in this sketch, it is only because they know the tune already.

MARK MORRIS, artistic director of the Mark Morris Dance Group, dancer, choreographer, conductor, and opera director

MARK MORRIS

Gertrude Stein Photographs

The Carl Van Vechten Collection

I worship Gertrude Stein's work. I staged *Four Saints in Three Acts* a while ago and read everything I could get my hands on, but these pictures of her in France during the war, are wonderful. It's a thrill to see her like this—she's even smiling in some, which is something I had never seen before.

She was careful never to smile in pictures, but here she is beaming. No one could say Gertrude Stein was attractive, but in many of these photographs she looks like a gorgeous man. Incredible!

YOKO ONO, multimedia artist and activist

YOKO ONO

Arnold Schoenberg, *Ode to Napoleon*, Op.41

ca. 1941

Sketch. John Cage, *Notations*

New York: Something Else Press, ca. 1969

John Cage, 0'00"

solo to be performed in anyway by anyone, 1962

Holograph, John Cage Music Manuscript Collection

Stefan Wolpe, letters to Irma Wolpe,

Baron/Wolpe Archive, 1956

John Cage was family to me, as well as to a few truly avant-garde composers of the time. We spent a lot of time together, mainly Cage inviting me to taste his mushroom salads he was always so proud of making.

It was really a wonderful surprise for me to see the book *Notations* in The New York Public Library. I never thought NYPL would carry a book of composition such as this one. *Notations* was the inspiration of John Cage, who also edited and published it. The book includes selections of important musical scores from a variety of mid-twentieth-century composers. Every composer in these pages was a rebel of their time. It's a superb book in so many ways—it shows how Cage was way ahead of his time and it was absolutely a groundbreaking book when it appeared in 1969. My score is in there too. As well as the Beatles' lyrics, when the classical music world still didn't think much of the boys yet. Just to scan the unique graphics that each composer decided to designate as a score is fascinating.

Jonathan Hiam, the curator, showed me a very rare Arnold Schoenberg score as well. It made me feel that I wanted to get in touch with my composer cousin in Tokyo, who is mad about Schoenberg, and I knew he would never have seen the originals of these scores.

Seeing Stefan Wolpe's handwritten writings reminded me of the days when we were close friends. He was the only prominent atonal composer we had in New York in those days, and I always thought he was so brave to keep his stance.

To see the different handwriting of the composers of these original scores was such a treat. Each handwriting tells you so much about the brilliant composers who created the history of music. Being able to hold the writings and manuscripts belonging to them was a rare experience. It gave me such a joy.

ERIC OWENS, bass/baritone opera singer

(previous pages)
ERIC OWENS in the stacks

ERIC OWENS

Photographed in the Stacks

ORHAN PAMUK , writer

ORHAN PAMUK

Voyage pittoresque de Constantinople et des rives du Bosphore, Antoine Ignace Melling (after)

engraving, 1819, Print Collection, Miriam and Ira D. Wallach Division of Art, Prints and Photographs

MARY LOUISE PARKER, actor

MARY LOUISE PARKER

"The Wild Swans at Coole," William Butler Yeats

holograph manuscript, unsigned and undated

CARYL PHILLIPS, writer

CARYL PHILLIPS

Photographs, Show Programs, Advertisements, and Letters Relating to Bert Williams

During 2002–3, I was fortunate to be able to spend a year as a fellow of the Dorthy and Lewis B. Cullman Center for Scholars and Writers at The New York Public Library, during which time I undertook research in the Library of the Performing Arts at Lincoln Center. My plan was to write a novel about the life of the early-twentieth-century comedian and entertainer Bert Williams. The task appealed to me not only because of the extraordinarily eventful life that Williams was privileged to live, but as a novelist I was fascinated to discover that this much-admired celebrity went out of his way to erase details of his personal history. He left no journals, no sheaves of letters, diaries, or the kind of material that a biographer might find useful. Therefore, as a novelist, my imagination was free to roam. In the comfort of The New York Public Library, I found photographs, old theater programs, posters, newspaper clippings, and letters written by those who knew Bert Williams; in short, a treasure trove of material that led me in all sorts of directions and eventually enabled me to complete the novel *Dancing in the Dark*.

One of the great blessings of the Internet age is the ease with which one can access research materials. Without ever leaving our homes we can, with a few judicious clicks on a keyboard, almost instantly peruse and print information that might in an earlier age have taken us hours, or even days, to locate. But information is not a substitute for knowledge. We learn in a more pedestrian and, in my own case, tactile fashion. I need to feel and touch primary research materials, and wonder by what route they arrived in the archives, and through how many pairs of hands they have passed. The amazing archives of The New York Public Library served as a spur to my imagination, and ushered me in the direction of reflection, which, in turn, led to knowledge; the archives provided me with an emotionally intimate connection with the past that the speedy information highway could never have offered.

We are all free to enter The New York Public Library and ask to see and hold manuscripts of novels, plays, songs, stories, or letters. We can look at original handwriting and corrected drafts, which allow us a window into the minds of those who have gone before us. We can hold history in our hands. At the end of my year as a fellow of the Library, I came to understand that there are two great miracles in the city of New York—Central Park and The New York Public Library; and both institutions are without gates and beckoning us to enter and reflect.

Sept 1918

The Midnight Sun

A SURE AND SAFE GUIDE THROUGH THE

NEW YORK SUBWAY

By

BERT WILLIAMS

OF THE

ZIEGFELD MIDNIGHT FROLIC

ATOP NEW AMSTERDAM THEATRE

who has submerged repeatedly,
always come to the surface safely;

who has visited the Catacombs of Rome;

who has visited the Mammoth Caves.

Published by Pusey Press, 136 West 42nd St., N. Y.

10c. a Copy

STAFF OF THE MIRIAM AND IRA D. WALLACH DIVISION OF ART, PRINTS AND PHOTOGRAPHS (l to r): Meredith Friedman, curatorial fellow; Stephen C. Pinson, assistant director and The Miriam and Ira D. Wallach Librarian for Art, Prints and Photographs, and The Robert B. Menschel curator of Photography; David Lowe, photography specialist

PHOTOGRAPHY COLLECTION STAFF

The Charlie Lucas Hubert's Museum Archive

1930s–1960s, Photography Collection,
The Miriam and Ira D. Wallach Division of
Art, Prints and Photographs

ubert's Museum, which opened in the 1920s on 42nd Street near Times Square, was a remnant of the nineteenth-century dime museum and one of the last existing sideshows in America. During its heyday, Hubert's was haunted by the likes of Bob Dylan, Tom Wolfe, and Andy Kaufman. Even Cole Porter once visited the museum to invite the bearded woman, Lady Olga, to a party at the Ritz Carlton. The Library's archive, acquired in 2010, is related to the final years of the museum, when it was managed by Richard Charles ("Charlie") Lucas, an African American performer and businessman originally from Chicago. A former Ringling Bros. Circus fire-eater, Lucas found success managing the kinds of African "jungle reviews" that he originally starred in, playing the African Prince "WooFoo." His wife, Mary "Woogie" Wigfall, eventually starred as Hubert's resident voodoo snake dancer, "Princess Sahloo." The archive includes photographs of Hubert's performers and exhibits, as well as other related materials such as manuscripts, correspondence, contracts, and log books. Of special note are Lucas's personal ledgers relating the day-to-day operations of the museum, a journal in which he recorded his dreams, a "grind tape" of the banter he used to

lure people into the show, and his personalized wooden storage trunk, painted bright red. The archive's pièce de résistance, however, is a group of vintage photographs by one of the most celebrated American photographers of the twentieth century, Diane Arbus (1923–1971).

Arbus sought out the museum in the late 1950s, when it was no longer considered "appropriate" for high- and lowbrows to mingle in the dark heart of New York City. At the time, Hubert's represented a generally, even perhaps willfully, overlooked aspect of American popular culture, right in the middle of a similarly forgotten and decayed Times Square. Arbus's photographs helped secure the legacy of Charlie Lucas and Hubert's Museum; they also offer important insights into Arbus's working methods and the development of her mature subject matter and style, particularly her ongoing fascination with and documentation of the dispossessed and marginalized communities for which she is now justly famous. The Library's archive contains the single most comprehensive collection of Arbus's photographs related to Hubert's Museum.

—Stephen Pinson, curator

JESSICA PIGZA , librarian, Rare Book Division

JESSICA PIGZA

Specimens of Wood Type

Hamilton Manufacturing Company, 1892

I find the Library's collection of wood type specimen books, with their outsized proportions and bold colors, to be fascinating, and I especially love sharing them with design students. I can't look through the pages of these volumes without imagining the boisterous nineteenth-century circus posters, newspaper headlines, advertisements, and other printed ephemera of the period that employed wood type to such memorable effect.

DARRYL PINCKNEY, novelist, playwright, and essayist

DARRYL PINCKNEY
GISSING ON THE TABLE

George Gissing, Holograph Diaries
Tuesday, Dec. 27, 1887–Nov. 8, 1902. 3 volumes

Whenever I visited Elizabeth Hardwick, I found on the coffee table in front of the red velvet sofa what she had been reading that day, what she had been working on. In the early stages of an essay or a story, Hardwick worked from her red sofa. She sank back into the cushions, legs crossed, and sketched out possible openings on legal pads—the way in was always the hardest thing for her—or jotted down quotations in notebooks. Usually she ended up more interested in what she was copying into her notebook than what she was coming up with on that legal pad.

I remember when Hardwick was thinking of writing about George Gissing, that depressed Victorian chronicler of masculine disappointment and the degradations of poverty. She was fascinated by the mess he'd made of his life. A brilliant scholarship student, he got kicked out for stealing, thus ruining forever his chances of an academic career. He'd stolen the money to give to the prostitute he'd fallen in love with and eventually married. Their life together in London was a disaster. She was a drunkard, and he couldn't have introduced her to anyone anyway. Because he was a writer, Gissing did not believe he had become déclassé, no matter how poor he was. But he lived in such dread of losing caste, as Hardwick put it, that for him to marry such an unsuitable girl was a self-destructive act. They parted; she died. In time, he found a second wife more ghastly than the first. Though sober, she raged, beat him, and he feared for the safety of his two boys. Eventually, she was locked up in an asylum and the boys farmed out. There was a French woman at the end, but Hardwick was somewhat unclear about her.

He died in France, attended by this French woman, I saw in *Gissing: A Life in Books* by John Halperin, which Hardwick had on the coffee table. She'd gone into the kitchen. We could get as drunk as the first Mrs. Gissing at these dinners, which were to me in my late youth also wondrous literary seminars. She'd been copying out lines from Gissing's novel that sold best in his lifetime, *The Ryecroft Papers:* "The thing is to get through life with as little suffering as possible." Though I'd not read Gissing at the time, I guessed that he was born to suffer and that that was why Hardwick found the line—and the several others she read out to me—hilarious.

Hardwick didn't write that essay on Gissing. And then a few years later, in 1981, she published in *The New York Review of Books* a short story, "Back Issues," in which an unidentified first-person woman narrator finds herself in The New York Public Library on 42nd Street, checking out everybody else. She has with her a notebook she just grabbed, "a nice object, cherry-colored, flecked with white and bound in a black strip: A-Plus Notebook made by Eaton Paper Division of Textron."

In this notebook, Hardwick's narrator has copied out lines about Gissing at his writing desk: "The trade of the damned." "This ink-stained world." "The reading public—oh, the reading public." I recall Hardwick saying that it gave her pleasure to bring into that story something of her abandoned Gissing studies, as well as other drifting literary impressions that she hadn't been able to make anything of. "What is to prevent your writing?"—her narrator has copied from "p. 79" of *New Grub Street.*

Back then, I thought that Gissing's talkative dramas about failed marriages and impecunious writers attracted the literary heroine, Elizabeth Hardwick, because they were so bleak, but now that I have read Gissing, now that I understand that she had no interest in being anybody's heroine, mine or literature's, I believe that much as she admired his misanthrope's realism, what most stirred her about Gissing was his will to work. Hardwick was touched by his toil. "What is to prevent? What is to prevent?"

In the reading room of the Berg Collection, with George Gissing's diaries: three medium-sized, softbound notebooks with black or marblelized covers. The pages are coated with his small, beautiful, and difficult handwriting. Sometimes I have to use a magnifying glass. The ink has turned the color of dried blood. The first entry was made in 1887, the year he published his first novel, and the last was written in 1903, the year he died, at the age of forty-six. From the first entry, December 27, 1887: "Today returned to Chapter I, which I must have rewritten six times, and again rewrote it." In the new year, 1888, he is reading *Great Expectations*. However. "Wrote nothing." And the next day, "Wrote nothing." Then: "Wrote from 3 to 9, but with no will; it must all be cancelled. Never mind."

Gissing's stoical, hard spirit seems to call forth the rain, the cold, the black fog at noon. It's all against him. "A wasted day. That sudden inability to work which often comes upon me, and is almost certain to do so just before any change in the ordering of my ways." He speaks of blank misery, of being incapable of work, of feeling suicidal. "Wed Jan 25. Suffered anguish worse than any I remember in the effort to compose. Ate nothing." So it goes, into spring. "Friday May 4. Feeling out of sorts. Wrote a page, then broke down." And I nearly broke down at that line. Hardwick searched out Gissing's forgotten novels, but I don't think she ever came to the reading room to peruse his diaries—the curator opens them for you on a felt cradle covered by green baize cloth, with something akin to a rosary or worry beads for a bookmark. Broke down. It is just the kind of line that would have made Hardwick laugh with sympathy.

Gissing produced rather conventional triple-deckers, yet he seems so modern in his alienation. He says at one point that although he has lived in London ten years, there isn't a single home where he, lonely and depressed, would be welcome; not one person who would receive him with good will. He was always thrown back on himself. His pen was a tool, another strenuous novel the means by which he fended off starvation, provided for his miserable little family. The books accumulate throughout his diaries—twenty-two novels and scores of bad short stories. He wrote literary journalism; he published a study of Dickens. Being Gissing, he was ripped off by his publishers for a long time.

Three notebooks, even in his tiny script, aren't much for the sixteen years that his diaries cover, but then he was busy, conceiving, sticking to it, recording that he was at his desk from seven to ten, then again after a walk from three to ten. His novels are spoken of as autobiographical, projections of himself. His steady labor earned him a solid reputation by the end of his short life. "I cannot stand obscurity."

I turn to a page in 1888 and his first wife's sodden death in a bare room means that a financial burden has been lifted. Gissing sets out for Paris. His economies are painful to read about. Never mind. It is June. He looks up Daudet's address, goes to his dignified stone building, with the windows all shuttered, and wonders if his hero could know about him. He spends days in the Louvre and looks for the celebrated actress Rachel's grave in the Jewish cemetery. By October, Paris has become distasteful to him, because his poverty means he has to lodge among working people in squalid streets.

Gissing's diaries change once the landscape of France rushes by the second-class windows of his train and his boat is on the sea. His pages become expansive. He feels a strange peace in Rome, is less happy in Florence, although the fig leaves there are only hung on nude statues with wire, not plastered on as they were in Rome. He was offended by the fig leaves daubed everywhere in the Sistine Chapel. Lectures at the Vatican's College of Propaganda were given in Latin. "A great variety of nationalities there: Arabs, Abyssinians, negroes, and c. I should like to know for certain: what kind of Latin such men speak."

But neither Rome nor Florence moved him as much as Naples, where he first landed. The braying donkeys, the scent of roasted chestnuts in the streets, the smoke of Vesuvius blowing white down the mountainside, Shelley's grave, the beautiful peasant girls in their long shawls—he carefully writes up his notes after a frugal lunch; he transcribes into his diary his hatched drawings of Naples Bay. The following year he, a classicist, went to Greece.

In his biography of Gissing—Hardwick's daughter, Harriet, gave me the books I associated with having been her mother's student—John Halperin tells us that after his trip to Italy, his work changed. He moved from harsh studies of social conditions and set about attacking Christianity, middle-class women, materialism, British imperialism, and at a time, in 1890, when he didn't have enough to eat, he managed to write *New Grub Street,* perhaps his most respected work. Typical of Gissing, he notes in his diary that his book is a success, yet he himself cannot afford to buy books.

The diaries continue, with the hell of his struggling to compose alternating with the hell of another unsuitable girl down in the kitchen. He was handsome and well built, meticulous in dress. In some diary entries, he is about to go mad with sexual need. He ended up with baffling women because he didn't feel he could court nice girls, so he settled for working-class girls who had a veneer of respectability. His French mistress was so respectable she wouldn't live with him without her mother. Toward the end of his days, he confessed that he was too unhappy to write. He had a hard death. His few friends loved him deeply.

I think of the conversations Hardwick and I can't have—about Gissing as an example of what she liked to call an innocent man, the sort of guy who wouldn't just have sex with a girl; he first had to convince himself that he was in love with her. I would want to point out how cheerfully, bravely, Chekhov faced poverty and took on his burdens. Chekhov and Gissing were contemporaries. But I can hear her protest that any comparison would be unfair to Gissing. His novels are dignified by the force of his ideas, but as literary achievements they don't compare to Chekhov's stories or plays.

I leave Gissing's notebooks on the table. The curator will tenderly box them up again. Every scratch on the battered covers whispers about his restlessness, his moving from place to place, his tally of hours at yet another writing desk. Long ago, Hardwick told me she kept a journal the summer after Robert Lowell left her, but she couldn't keep it up. It was not interesting, she insisted. I saw it, a large brown leather-bound album full of her big, neat handwriting. But after Hardwick's death, her daughter found no trace of it. O, the reading public.

MARTHA PLIMPTON, actor and singer

MARTHA PLIMPTON

Beadle's Dime Novels

Dime novels are the beginning of pop. Some people might tend to look down on pop culture, or else appreciate it with a sort of phony irony. But we all secretly love it in a sort of queasy, visceral way that some of us like to vivisect in public. Pop shows us our lives as we are living them, which can sometimes seem a grotesque diversion. Looking at dime novels, with their lurid take on our already violent history—cowboys and Indians, white slavery scares, out-of-wedlock sex, outlaws, "justifiable homicide"—you find another history within a history. Never mind what really happened at, say, Little Big Horn. What we wish had happened says so much more about *who we really were* then. Dime novels give us a chronicle of the American imagination at a time of fantastic change, when everything started moving at a previously unimaginable rate of speed. Written in splashy, immediate, Technicolor style, they were perfect for the bored, frustrated women of the leisure classes who had magazine subscriptions and their own private visions of Manifest Destiny. Mass-produced on cheap stock, then collated in paperback form, the stories were also ideally suited for rapid consumption by antsy city kids—call them punks—itching to escape their stifling urban confines to become their own men in the wide-open "Wild West." They were thin and easy to hide in the folds of your skirts. Or to conceal on the inside of a lesson book. Fancy ladies and dirty-faced urchins generally get excited by the same things, anyway, but like the pulp fiction that came early the next century, dime novels are wonderfully democratic without being kind. They're perfectly, bluntly, wholly American.

JOSÉ MANUEL PRIETO, novelist, translator, and scholar

JOSÉ MANUEL PRIETO

A RESERVOIR OF BOOKS

El ingenioso hidalgo Don Quixote de la Mancha [Parte 1]
Miguel de Cervantes Saavedra
Madrid: Por J. de la Cuesta, 1605

"La lotería en Babilonia"
Jorge Luis Borges
first edition, holograph, undated

Jorge Luis Borges imagined the library as a whole universe—a way of expressing the total experience of the library, the feeling of veneration aroused by the books it contains, the summits of knowledge enclosed within its walls. One of his stories, "The Library of Babel," begins with the now-famous line, "The Universe (which others call the Library) . . ." and goes on to offer this image: "an indefinite and perhaps infinite number of hexagonal galleries, with vast air shafts between, surrounded by very low railings."[1] An odd description, I've always thought, its geometric and highly predictable design inspiring me with dislike. Difficult to think of it as a dwelling place. And I certainly can't imagine myself living eternally in a library. I would miss everything I find outside, in people and their stories.

Though, to tell the truth, if there is a place on earth where I've spent interminable hours, it is libraries, working in them, doing research in their collections, writing. This is an old and unbroken habit. For the first of my novels, I spent many long days in the heated halls of the venerable Public Library of Saint Petersburg, which have left me with the fondest of memories. While working on another, I plowed indefatigably through books that had emerged from the fearsome *spetskhran*, the place in the Lenin State Library where books on the index of the Soviet censors are kept. One summer, I spent several mornings in the Bibliothèque Nationale in Paris reading the only available copy of the *Turkish Letters* by Ogier Ghiselin de Busbecq, ambassador from Austria to the court of Suleiman the Magnificent, and highly absorbing reading it was.

But of all the libraries where I've worked, I maintain a truly personal relationship only with The New York Public Library. I spent a year there as a fellow of the Dorthy and Lewis B. Cullman Center for Scholars and Writers in 2005 and it is one of the few places in Manhattan where I feel truly at home. When a text I'm writing starts putting up obstacles or the solution to a chapter isn't coming readily, I know I can resolve the matter simply by going to work in the Main Reading Room on the third floor, in the left wing (never the right), beneath an ever-cheerful sky. And from that sky, that painted sky, the solution miraculously descends, the phrase that rescues me from my quagmire.

I think of the Library as a tranquil sea on whose banks I come to sit and ponder my next book, an image rooted in the historical fact that this library is perhaps unique in the world in having been built atop a former reservoir, the Croton Distributing Reservoir. But I, born and raised on an island and therefore a maritime creature, prefer to see it as a sea, an ocean of books. Not the entire universe, as in Borges: only a vast sea.

One morning a short while ago, I had further confirmation of just how rich a sea it is when a librarian placed in my hands the first edition of the *Ingenioso hidalgo Don Quijote de la Mancha* by Miguel de Cervantes, the famous Juan Cuesta edition of 1605. I leafed through it in rapt wonderment: a true miracle to be seeing this perfectly preserved folio here in Manhattan. A copy, I thought, that could have belonged to Cervantes himself; those annotations in the margin made by an unknown hand . . . And half an hour later, swimming only a few strokes further into this sea, I found myself religiously inclined over the manuscript of "La lotería de Babilonia," ("The Lottery of Babel"), the famous story by Jorge Luis Borges. A schoolboy's notebook, its graph paper covered in minuscule handwriting, "insect tracks" I could decipher without too much effort, despite all the crossing out and emendation. Nothing is more comforting, I thought, nothing reconciles you more to your own struggle to find the right word than seeing such deletions and corrections on the text of a classic.

Curiously, Cervantes and Borges come together in another of the latter's texts, "Pierre Menard, autor del Quijote," a work, like all of Borges's works, that emerged from his long peregrinations through the library, his highly attentive readings. Borges imagines Menard rewriting the Spanish classic. Not the entire book, just two of its chapters and part of another one. Two citations from the story will explain the idea Borges had of his own writing: (1) "Cervantes' text and Menard's are verbally identical, but the second is almost infinitely richer." (2) "Menard's fragmentary *Quixote* is more subtle than Cervantes'." For Borges, the rewritten, recombined book is superior to the original.

By a strange affinity, through my study of engineering, which made me familiar with the laws of combinatorics and Boolean logic, and through my reading of Borges himself, I've always practiced a kind of writing that relies greatly on libraries. In certain of my fictional texts I've made profuse use of citations. My point is that I see the library not as a passive depository of books, but as a generative mass that *alone* is capable of writing the best works, those that are most astute and penetrating. In this I am a bit like Georges Perec, another great admirer of Borges and the inventor of the "story-making machine."

It seems to me therefore that as we celebrate the centennial of The New York Public Library, in fact we are celebrating the jubilee of what may be this city's greatest author: the Library itself. Its building understood as a living being in whose belly, in whose reservoir of books, swim all texts, all treatises, all novels, those already written and those yet to come, joining and recombining. We need only sit on its shores and watch them flash, sparkle, and mirror each other in this great body of water.

Translated from the Spanish by Esther Allen

1. English translations of Borges's works cited here are from *Labyrinths*, edited by Donald Yates and James Irby (New York: New Directions, 1962; reissued 2007 with a preface by William Gibson). Both passages cited were translated by James E. Irby.

FRANCINE PROSE, novelist

(previous pages)
FRANCINE PROSE

FRANCINE PROSE

BRASSAÏ

Photographs of the Villa Lante, Brassaï

gelatin silver prints, 1962

A Portfolio of Ten Photographs, Brassaï

gelatin silver prints, 1973, Photography Collection,
The Miriam and Ira D. Wallach Division of
Art, Prints and Photographs

The Library has everything! That's what I often find myself saying, taking advantage of the most marginally appropriate conversational excuses to rave about what The New York Public Library has in its collection. I say: There's nothing you want that they don't have—at least in the way of books, manuscripts, photos, scrolls, maps, magazines, and literary ephemera.

In fact, they have plenty of things you probably never even knew you wanted. For example, let's say that you long to hold in your hand the paw of Charles Dickens's much-loved cat, Bob. The Berg Collection possesses this peculiar object, which Dickens, like many of his fellow Victorians, had made into a letter opener after his pet passed away.

During the year I spent as a fellow at the Dorthy and Lewis B. Cullman Center for Scholars and Writers, among the happiest of my life, there was nothing I needed that the Library couldn't provide to help with my research for my book, *The Lives of the Muses*. Would I like to look at Lewis Carroll's portrait of Alice Liddell as the beggar child? It just so happened that the Berg Collection owns the presentation copy that Carroll himself hand-tinted and framed for Alice, his child inspiration.

The Library's generous resources continue to amaze me. Working on a novel loosely based on an incident in the life of the French-Hungarian photographer Brassaï, I discover that the Photography Collection has original prints of a little-known series that Brassaï took of Italian gardens, as well as a limited-edition volume of some of his iconic images of Paris at night.

I never know quite what moves me most: the presence, the actuality of the things themselves, or the simple fact that they exist in a public institution built at a time when the spirit of our nation was animated by an almost holy belief in progress, self-improvement, and the power of education. You can still feel something of that belief. Just spend an hour in the Rose Main Reading Room, watching the readers who use it: old and young, male and female, native New Yorkers and people from all over the world. I boast about the Library as if it were mine, and part of what's so thrilling is the fact that it is. NYPL belongs to the people.

You don't even need a borrowing card, or citizenship, or papers. It is almost unbelievable how much there is in the Library to see and touch—and to read. The only things required are the curiosity and the desire that every human creature would have, if only we were encouraged.

ANNIE PROULX, novelist, journalist, and short-story writer

ANNIE PROULX

Henry David Thoreau, *The Dispersion of Seeds*

holograph notes, unsigned and undated

The 1861 photograph of Henry David Thoreau (1817–62) showing his long, homely face with a repulsive ruff of neck whiskers, the beseeching eyes, is the face of a man who was dying and knew it. The family health was fragile; Thoreau's older sister died of tuberculosis, and his beloved brother, John, cut himself while shaving and succumbed to lockjaw.

Thoreau's ideas and behavior—transcendentalism and a belief that physical work was unnatural—ran against the New England moral grain that regarded the natural world as a source of raw exploitation, and exalted labor as the highest moral good. He was likely a bit of a fool to his neighbors and to early critics. But in the 150 years since his death his treatises and essays have been shaped into monoliths of American literature.

The Dispersion of Seeds lay dormant for 125 years after Thoreau's death, until, in 1993, it was edited by Bradley P. Dean and published by Island Press as *Faith in Seeds*. This Thoreau was not the standard-bearer of civil disobedience, nor the self-seeking nature boy, but Thoreau the field scientist whose study was the forests and fields of Concord, Massachusetts. Psychologically the observation of forest seeds and species successions may have been attractive to the mortally ill man who never married and had no children. There is often tenderness in his sentences when he describes the fresh legions of tiny pine or oak seedlings that sprang up in local pastures. Thoreau worked on the manuscript in his final years of life and it reveals his profound powers of observation of the natural world, his obsessive attention to the rhythms of untamed life.

The section that deals with succession of forest tree species from seed was a daring refutation of the then universal belief that trees sprang into existence spontaneously. But Thoreau was sure. For many years he had watched forest seed dispersal and compiled thousands of precise notes detailing the minutiae of interactions between pines and oaks, seedlings and humans. In addition he kept endless lists of times of tree leaf-out, bird migrations, fruit ripeness, flower bloom, the appearance of insects, and much more. This kind of work is not easy, requiring years of diligence in charting and interpreting natural phenomena. Thoreau was an intent observer of tree habits of seed production, noting when and how the seeds were dispersed: falling to the ground, carried on the wind, portaged by birds in beaks and stomachs, by clinging to the fur of animals, by floating in streams and rivers, by sliding on snow. In his final two years of life he read and absorbed Darwin's *Origin of Species* and was the first American man of letters to embrace Darwin's ideas. His writing style was lucid and elegant; *Faith in Seeds* remains very readable.

All of this is important, but there is another reason I like and admire this manuscript. In these pages I find the New England of my childhood and my maternal ancestors, a whole cupboard of olfactory and visual memories, even childhood games. My mother's family has lived in Connecticut since 1635, many generations familiar with New England woods and fields. In the 1930s and '40s my cousins and I played in and with the local flora. Our elders knew all the plants and their habits and passed on that invaluable lore. We gathered beechnuts and butternuts, chestnuts, and sometimes hickories, picked hazelnuts, whose invigorating perfume is still vivid in my mind. We gathered dandelion greens, fiddlehead fern shoots, "sour grass" (wild sorrel), marsh marigolds, wild onions, "skoke" (aka pokeweed), which has poisonous roots and berries, though the properly cooked young leaves are a delicious spring green. We gathered rose hips, wild strawberries, raspberries, blueberries and huckleberries, roamed the old abandoned orchards gathering wormy apples, unaware that the soil was saturated with lead arsenate from nineteenth-century orchard spray. We played with plants—the flowers of bindweed for ladies' skirts, four-leaf clovers for luck, mallow fruits for the tiny segmented "cheeses," milkweed pods and dandelion fluff for airborne parachutes. My mother pointed out ginseng plants, which she had dug up in her youth, selling the roots for pin money, and told us about gathering milkweed pods to sell to the government for use in kapok life jackets.

Thoreau seemed to have a special fondness for the floating downy seeds of thistles, milkweed, and especially the dandelions. He noted dandelions going to seed around the 9th of May in Concord and wrote, "By the 4th of June they are *generally* gone to seed in the rank grass. You see it dotted with a thousand downy spheres, and children now make ringlets of their crispy stems."[1] A half page of the manuscript is missing here, but if Thoreau described the making of those ringlets in the missing paragraph, I know well what he would have written, for my sisters and I blew away the "downy spheres" and then, with our sharp little-girl thumbnails, slit the stem into four or five strands. We then put the stem ends in our mouths and pulled them through our lips two or three times. Miraculously the limp stem strands curled up into tight ringlets. It was such an amazing transformation we never tired of this play. Even the lingering bitter taste of the stems was worth it. Today, of course, lawn maniacs spend millions of dollars on dandelion eradication chemicals to kill the plants. What a world we live in!

So many of the tree and plant species that Thoreau regarded and watched as though they were children are now gone. In his innocence he never suspected the horrific damage Americans would do to their forests through casual imports, unbridled cutting, and poor "management" practices. The woods of Concord in his time are not our woods. Outraged, he once chided a neighbor who had cut down his pine woodlot, and when young oaks followed in succession, burned them off and planted rye. "So he trifles with Nature. I am chagrined for him. That he should call himself an agriculturist! He needs to have a guardian placed over him."[2] But just think what has happened to the trees Thoreau knew.

The chestnut (*Castanea dentata*) once made up one-third of the eastern forest. It was the most useful tree then known, made into house siding, floors, fine furniture, fence rails, and even, in Thoreau's time, railroad sleepers. In my mother's lifetime it still grew here and there, but was already dying from the dreadful chestnut blight. Thoreau didn't know about the blight, which entered American forests forty years after his death, but he did worry about the excessive cutting of this wonder tree. "It is now comparatively scarce and costly; and there is danger, if we do not take unusual care, that this tree will become extinct here."[3] That might have happened, but the blight got there first. Around 1900 the killer came into the United States either through infected imported lumber or through the efforts of tree hybridizers wanting bigger chestnuts and who thought to get them by crossing the native tree with the Chinese chestnut. Alas, the Chinese variety carried the fatal fungus. Within a human generation millions of American chestnuts were gone. Such was the vigor of the native tree that it still keeps putting up new growth from its old roots, young trees which grew to a certain size and then succumb to the blight.

The American elm was the distinctive tree of New England, its graceful wineglass shape found throughout the forests and along the streets of a thousand small towns. But cabinet makers imported English elm for its beautiful patterned veneers, and those English logs were infested with bark beetles carrying a vicious fungus later called "Dutch elm disease." There were still elms during my childhood, but as I walked home from school I saw the sidewalks and byways of New England become sun-scalded strips, with enormous stumps all that remained of the exquisite elms.

I can remember gathering fallen butternuts at a very early age with my mother. The chocolate-colored nuts looked as though they were wearing velvet jackets, but they were terrifically sticky and stained hands and cloths. The velvet jackets had a distinctive, rich butternut odor a little like almonds toasted in sweet butter, the promise of the delicious chambered meats inside. In my lifetime the butternut contracted a fungus that developed into a fatal canker. Experts link the demise of the butternut to air pollution. It was the first tree on the Endangered Species candidate list. Air pollution, acid rain, over-harvesting, a flood of foreign fungi and insects, monoculture, domestic stock grazing, climate change, and a hundred other causes are bringing American forests to the ground. And now the sugar maple is damaged by acid rain and the lodgepole pines of the West have become thousands of miles of dead trees on steep slopes, the perfect recipe for erosion and flood. Almost every tree species is approaching a watershed pandemic situation. I am glad Thoreau was spared the brutal knowledge of what would happen to his beloved forests.

1. H.D. Thoreau, *Faith in Seeds,* Island Press, Washington, D.C. 1993, p. 83
2. Ibid., p. 173
3. Ibid., p. 126

LISA RANDALL, author and professor of physics at Harvard University

LISA RANDALL

Andreas Cellarius

Atlas Coelestis, seu Harmonia Microcosmica

1661

LOU REED, musician, singer, songwriter, and photographer

LOU REED

"The Rationale of Verse," Edgar Allan Poe
manuscript page
1843

DAVID REMNICK, author and editor of *The New Yorker*

DAVID REMNICK

MEMORY BOXES

Speak, Memory, Vladimir Nabokov

holograph of changes made to *Conclusive Evidence*
on 404 index cards

Vladimir Nabokov and his wife, Vera, are buried side by side in a tomb in the Cimetière de Clarens, in Montreux, Switzerland. The headstone resembles the headboard on a marital bed. And yet, it is hard not to think of Nabokov's true resting place as the series of pale gray boxes found in the Berg Collection of The New York Public Library. Here resides not the bones but the spirit's remains: the countless butterfly drawings in colored pencil; journal accounts of consciousness (a "butterfly dream": 23 Nov. 1964, 6:45 a.m.); a paperback copy of *Ulysses* with marginal notes working out the time sequences and Dublin wanderings of Leopold Bloom; a worn softcover copy of the Charles I. Weir translation of *Madame Bovary* with looping tendrils of corrections and exasperated deletions ("looking frowningly" is replaced by "scowling"; on page 106, Nabokov simply gives up on Weir and writes in the margin: "idiot"). The Berg Collection contains countless scraps of the Nabokovian imagination: a genealogical chart of the family; a strange notebook sketching out metrical schemes of Russian poems as if they were chess problems; a diagram of the five-part scheme for the late novel *Ada*.

Nabokov, who had learned to be an astringent grader while teaching European and Russian literature to undergraduates at Cornell, marked up his copy of *Fifty-five Short Stories from* The New Yorker, *1940–1950* by assigning letter grades to each. For the sake of a kinder posterity, suffice to say that Nabokov did not grade on the curve. Amid a blizzard of C's and other middling marks, he handed out one A—to "The Lottery" by Shirley Jackson—and two A pluses—to "A Perfect Day for Bananafish" by J.D. Salinger, and "Colette" by Vladimir Vladimirovich Nabokov.

It is hard to argue with Nabokov's self-admiration. "Colette" is based on a childhood journey from St. Petersburg to Biarritz and is obsessed, as is so much in Nabokov, with a remembered incident—in this case, a brief affection for a young girl—and a single memory's capacity to reappear at any time:

"The leaves mingle in my memory with the leather of her shoes and gloves, and there was, I remember, some detail in her attire (perhaps a ribbon on her Scottish cap, or the pattern of her stockings) that reminded me then of the rainbow spiral in a glass marble. I still seem to be holding that wisp of iridescence, not knowing exactly where to fit it in, while she runs with her hoop ever faster around me and finally dissolves among the slender shadows cast on the gravelled path by the interlaced arches of its border."

Most writers are amused by the idea of archives. The idea that a library would pay a fortune for discarded drafts and attract eager scholars willing to spend their days poring over them strikes them as funny. "Most critics have nothing intelligent to say about my good stuff, the stuff I choose to publish," Philip Roth has said. "Why do they want to spend time with my trash?"

If the Bergian boxes are conclusive evidence, then Nabokov left behind very little garbage for the scholars. What failures he had in the midst of writing, he usually erased or destroyed. Not long ago, some friends at the Berg collection brought out the casket in which they kept the manuscript of *Speak, Memory.* In countless interviews, Nabokov patiently described his work fetishes, the most striking of which was his habit of writing on index cards. He did not have available to him the computer-age ability to cut and paste, to move blocks of text with the press of a button. He shuffled the deck.

The cards are encased in clear, protective plastic, but it was not long before I flipped to the passage that never leaves me. It has always seemed to me Nabokov's credo. Like Joseph Brodsky, who was reared in the same city, if under radically different circumstances, Nabokov is a poet of time:

"I confess I do not believe in time," he writes in the early stages of *Speak, Memory.* "I like to fold my magic carpet, after use, in such a way as to superimpose one part of the pattern upon another. Let visitors trip. And the highest enjoyment of timelessness—in a landscape selected at random—is when I stand among rare butterflies and their food plants. This is ecstasy, and behind the ecstasy is something else, which is hard to explain. It is like a momentary vacuum into which rushes all that I love. A sense of oneness with sun and stone. A thrill of gratitude to whom it may concern—to the contrapuntal genius of human fate or to tender ghosts humoring a lucky mortal."

FRANK RICH, journalist and author

(previous pages)
FRANK RICH with the set model
for *Follies* (detail above)

FRANK RICH

Set Model for *Follies* Designed by Boris Aronson

Billy Rose Theatre Division

1971

y love affair with The New York Public Library began when I was still only an aspiring New Yorker. As a stage-struck high school student in Washington, D.C., I would scheme to get to the city on weekends to see plays, then would repair to the old Donnell branch during any spare hours to take a stab at doing homework that would be due when I (sadly) reported back to real life on Monday morning. The Donnell was less intimidating to a young out-of-town interloper than 42nd Street, and even a biology assignment seemed romantic when puzzled over in a library looking out on the Museum of Modern Art.

But my most extended interaction with NYPL came some two decades later, when I spent several years in the mid-1980s working on research projects at the Performing Arts Library at Lincoln Center—often for weeks at a time, and on some days from the moment the doors opened until the moment the last malingers were politely evicted. Back then I was the theater critic of *The New York Times,* and one of those projects was my first book, *The Theatre Art of Boris Aronson* (Knopf, 1987). It was a chronicle of a groundbreaking scenic designer whose career extended from post-revolutionary Russia in the early 1920s to the mid-century Broadway of Arthur Miller, Tennessee Williams, Elia

Kazan, Jerome Robbins, and Stephen Sondheim—with stops along the way as various as New York's avant-garde Yiddish theaters, the early stage extravaganzas of Radio City Music Hall, The Group Theater, and American Ballet Theater. (Aronson's final production had been Mikhail Baryshnikov's *Nutcracker* for the ABT, just across the Lincoln Center plaza.)

I never met Aronson (1898–1980), who had died before I embarked on the book. Working in collaboration with his widow and creative partner, Lisa Aronson, I had to reconstruct not just his life but, more importantly, the intense process by which he created dozens of landmark sets for the theater. Particularly in the commercial arena of Broadway, where Aronson did most of his greatest work, sets are among the most ephemeral (and least understood) elements of any production. The actual sets are destroyed after a show closes. The drawings and models that dictated the design may have fallen into the hands of private collectors, or been given away, or lost. Nearly as scarce is the written record—the letters and memos and even telegrams (ah, those were the days!) that would fly back and forth among a play's director, author, producer, and designer as they adjudicated a myriad of complex artistic decisions.

Luckily, Lisa Aronson had preserved all she could of her husband's archive, much of which she had or would bestow upon the Performing Arts Library. The papers of many of his most important collaborators were also available there, so that I could fill in the never chronicled, and in some cases forgotten, history of some of the American theater's most lustrous, yet by definition evanescent, achievements. This was at times arduous detective work, but I was never on my own. The Library's knowledgeable and devoted staff guided me every step of the way—as they did any and all visitors, however difficult or modest the task that brought them there. I thank again Betty Corwin, Thor Wood, Dorothy Swerdlove, and Diane Bruning—stalwarts of the Library at that time who live very much in my memory a quarter-century later.

The Performing Arts Library had particular meaning to the Aronsons. After Boris Aronson's death, it mounted, in 1981, the first comprehensive exhibit of his work—one of the many important shows that are central to the institution's history. Somewhat more surprisingly, the Library also directly influenced one of Aronson's most famous designs—for the original Broadway production of *Company,* the 1970 musical, now recognized as a classic, that was a career-changing breakthrough for Sondheim, the director Harold Prince, and the choreographer Michael Bennett.

Company, as written by the playwright George Furth, was a sardonic (and at the time controversial) look at marriage in modern Manhattan. Aronson's assignment was to capture the discordant ambiance of contemporary New York in a single set. He did so abstractly, with what he called a "jungle gym for actors"—a multi-platform, two-level sculpture of scaffolding that was a throwback to the Constructivist style of his formative artistic years in Russia. The biggest literal influence on the set was the reference reading room of the Performing Arts Library, which Aronson discovered on a walking tour of New York as he was thinking through his design. What caught his eye was the glassed-in steel-edged frame of the room—"a hospital for books," as he called it, which to him epitomized a city in which "apartments are like hospitals, antiseptic environments without privacy."

The model of that set now resides at Lincoln Center, appropriately enough—though that reading room has since been remodeled. But my favorite artifact in the Performing Arts Library collection is Aronson's model for his set for his next collaboration with Sondheim, Prince, and Bennett—*Follies* (1971), a musical about a reunion of aging Follies performers in their old Broadway theater the night before it is razed for a parking lot. Aronson's design, like the show itself, is almost unbearably poignant. The once grand show-business palace is already half-demolished, a ghostly ruin from a vanished time and vanished culture, now abandoned by a city that never stops reinventing itself.

That Aronson's work of Proustian art remains in safekeeping for anyone to see at the Performing Arts Library—long after the original set of *Follies* was carted off to the junkyard—is just one of the countless reasons why The New York Public Library, in all its iterations, is an irreplaceable and heroic caretaker of civilization as it has been practiced in our great city.

JOSH RITTER, musician, singer, songwriter, and author, holding Virginia Woolf's cane

JOSH RITTER

"Ego Dominus Tuus," William Butler Yeats,
from *The Wild Swans at Coole*
holographed manuscript
1918–1919

There is the reading, of course. That is the given reason for going to a library.

But I think that there's another. I think that sometimes we go to libraries simply to be surrounded by and reminded of the enormity of human experience. Wandering down the aisles, our hands trailing absently from spine to spine, there are moments in a library when the collected and collective voices of our entire human history come crashing down around us like a wave, and, catching us up, prove to us that we are, individually, still a part of something sublime, chaotic, unknowable, and huge. As more and more of our lives are lived down some cyber-age rabbit hole mistaking information-on-demand for human knowledge, it's a relief at times to walk physically through the jumbles, the conundrums, the mutterings, and shoutings of a million other souls across the centuries and to share in their amazement at the world we live in. It is good to be able to walk in wonder, if not understanding, among the constellations and chemical reactions, shipwrecks, high towers, songbirds, night sounds, saints, pin-up girls, jungle adventurers, and a billion other people and things. It is good to know that others went before us, thought before us, questioned before us, blazed before us, and then winked out, leaving behind their words as proof of their passing.

Finally, it is good to be reminded by the sheer voluminous presence of all of these searching books that even with all that we think we know, mystery endures and whatever magic there is in life continues to live on, not in our answers, but in our questions.

The Yeats poem "Ego Dominus Tuus," the original copy of which I was able to hold in my hands at The New York Public Library, says this:

Those men that in their writings are most wise
Own nothing but their blind, stupefied hearts.

Many, many thanks to The New York Public Library and to all who work there. May it and they continue to inspire and confound us for hundreds of years to come.

RADIO CITY ROCKETTES, representatives of the world-famous dance troupe

(previous pages and above)
RADIO CITY ROCKETTES in the Rose Main Reading Room

RADIO CITY ROCKETTES

The Deborah, Jonathan F.P. Samuel Priest,
and Adam R. Rose Main Reading Room

PHILIP ROTH, writer

PHILIP ROTH

SAUL BELLOW

Mr. Sammler's Planet, Saul Bellow

notebooks, manuscripts, typescripts, and galley proofs

1961–1970

When you move from your final manuscript into long, beautiful galleys like these, you're able to read the book fresh and in its entirety for the first time in years, to read it not like the book you're working on that keeps defeating you but finally as the realized book, wholly and miraculously imagined. Suddenly lapses of thought, excesses of description, errors of style, and even of conception can become clear to you, just because of the change in format. Look at Saul's galleys—crammed with his handwriting at the top and bottom margins, changes excitedly set down that only sprang to mind when he got to see the finished novel set in type. This process of moving from your own typed pages with their all-too-familiar typeface to the printer's fresh new pages seems to spring the lock on the most felicitous additions that have otherwise remained inaccessible to you for the previous five years. I'm surprised to see how small these little notebooks are in which he got started in longhand. Beginning a project, for most of us, is usually the most agonizing moment—a moment that can last from six months to a year or longer. These little handwritten notebooks are the beginning of the process that ends in the corrected galley pages. All the *Sturm und Drang* of day-to-day composition is enacted between the first tentative sentences laid down here in longhand and those glorious last-minute inspirations evoked by the neat typography of the complete work in print.

OLIVER SACKS, physician and author

(previous pages)

OLIVER SACKS studying a first edition of *Systema naturae*, Carolus Linnaeus (1735)

OLIVER SACKS

On the Origin of Species by Means of Natural Selection, Charles Darwin
first edition, 1859

On the Origin of Species by Means of Natural Selection was published in London on the 24th of November 1859. Prior to its publication, it was almost universally assumed that the animals and plants on earth had been unchanged since the day of Creation, and that the earth itself was only 6,000 years old. Longer time scales had been suggested by some geologists, especially Lyell, who had been forced to the realization that the earth might be hundreds of millions of years older than this. A few naturalists, looking at the fossil record, felt that evolution of a sort had occurred, but this was envisioned as the rolling out of a predetermined plan, a blueprint or design whereby animals of higher and higher order would emerge at appointed times, culminating in man, the only animal worthy to be possessed of a divine soul. There was no room, in the unfolding of such a plan, for chance or accident.

Darwin's vision—of natural selection acting on entire populations, favoring the fittest, expunging others in an amoral, relentless selection—was provocative in the extreme, and the book's entire first edition of 1,250 copies sold out on the day of publication. (Its publisher, John Murray, quickly ordered a second edition, and Darwin went on to revise the book a number of times, incorporating responses to his readers and additional ammunition for his theory.)

Holding this first edition, one of the original 1,250 copies, in my hands gives me an almost physical sense of Darwin himself and of the mental world of 1859, the mental world that he was about to explode. It makes me wonder too who else might have handled this particular copy. Who bought it on that day 151 years ago? A naturalist, like Darwin himself? A theologian? Did the book produce a sudden revelation, an epiphany, or a more gradual illumination? Or conflict, denial, a howl of execration? No other book (except, perhaps, Copernicus's *De Revolutionibus Orbium Coelestium*—though that, published in Latin, had a much smaller readership) has ever challenged conventional thinking in so radical and abrupt a fashion. Darwin's "dangerous idea" (as Daniel Dennett put it) evoked every possible reaction.

But the book I am holding bears no signature, no hint of its provenance. We do not know whose hands it passed through—or what reactions it elicited—before it came to The New York Public Library. The appearance of this book—not fancy, bound in simple green cloth, and a little worse for the wear—belies its power, the fact that it was an intellectual hydrogen bomb destined to reshape the ideas of every thinking man on the planet, challenging the whole notion of order as it was conceived in Darwin's time. Minutely and relentlessly laid out (Darwin had the skills of a lawyer and a novelist as well as a scientist), the *Origin* is also lyrical, nowhere more than in the beautiful words with which it ends:

> *There is grandeur in this view of life, with its several powers, having been originally breathed into a few forms or into one; and that, whilst this planet has gone cycling on according to the fixed law of gravity, from so simple a beginning endless forms most beautiful and most wonderful have been, and are being, evolved.*

ROBERT SILVERS, editor of *The New York Review of Books*

ROBERT SILVERS

Les Essais de Michel Seigneur de Montaigne

1595

Montaigne's last years before his death in 1592 were taken up with a large-scale revision of the Essays. *Two books of* Essays *were published in 1580, and a third book followed in 1588 with the first two books heavily rewritten and considerably enlarged. His own copy of this expanded edition (called the "Bordeaux Copy") has revisions in his hand throughout, with indications of inserts that are sometimes many pages in length. The posthumous edition of 1595, overseen by his disciple Marie de Gournay, incorporated these changes with relative fidelity.*

—Charles Rosen, "The Genius of Montaigne," *The New York Review,* February 14, 2008

The beautifully printed and bound 1595 edition is the one I saw at the New York Public Library. I was shown the book, which is usually held in the Rare Book Division, in The George Arents Collection on Tobacco. (Is this because he wrote, "I fear a stuffy atmosphere and avoid smoke like the plague"?)

Small, abstract ornaments break up the text. It is a marvelous format for a collection of essays that are quietly subversive, charming, and profound at the same time.

ZADIE SMITH, writer

ZADIE SMITH

Mr. William Shakespeares Comedies, Histories & Tragedies

First Folio Edition, 1623

ST. VINCENT, musician

(previous pages)

ST. VINCENT with Claude Debussy's autographed manuscript of "Les Papillions"

ST. VINCENT

"Les Papillons," Claude Debussy

holograph, 1881 (?)

I was struck by Debussy's autographed manuscript of "Les Papillions," a gift for his muse, Mme. Vasnier, a married woman some years his senior. The personal inscription, in his swirling floral penmanship, reads: "To Madame Vanier [sic] who alone has a voice light enough to sing songs about butterflies. The Butterflies. Pantoum by Th. Gautier. Set aflutter by Ach. Debussy."

What most charmed me was this clumsy misspelling of his muse's name in his inscription, and the hasty squiggle on the last measure of the first page; a minor transcription mistake, a relic of a second thought, and a reminder that the artist was once very much alive. This misspelled name, along with the adherence to conventional poetic form, helps date the piece to 1881, when Debussy was still a young man and up-and-comer. By the end of his life, the composer would write twenty-seven pieces for Mme. Vasnier. "Les Papillions," however, would remain unknown to the public until its premiere in 1962 by Julliard trained soprano Billie Lynn Daniel.

There is such a tenderness and compassion in Debussy's work. Such a delicate hand must be, in my estimation, the indicator of a deeply romantic soul. Getting to hold this inscribed score in my hand and pour over the minute details, from penmanship to fluttery, effervescent nuance of note, helped confirm this suspicion. It reminds me that the motivation behind so much music, from the revered masters to the pop singers, is often: *get the one you love to love you back.*

WESLEY STACE, musician and writer

WESLEY STACE

My Dog Tulip, J.R Ackerley

holograph and typescript notes and drafts, unsigned and undated
with undated photograph of "Queenie"

azing at me with soft, glowing eyes, she kissed my cheek," remembers the narrator, recalling a night-time visit when his lover was "young and irresponsible and our love was new." By the book's end, she is his "burning bitch, burning in her beauty and heat." The metaphor isn't harsh, or even a metaphor: she's a dog.

My Dog Tulip (1956) is ostensibly the story of the relationship, platonic, between the British writer J.R. Ackerley and Queenie, his silver German shepherd, here renamed. She was also the star of Ackerley's only novel, *We Think the World of You.* In Queenie, he found his great subject matter; through her, he expressed the inexpressible.

When I picked up the reissue of *Tulip,* my girlfriend had a rather neurotic, extremely beautiful, rake-thin German shepherd named Grey. Queenie and Grey, separated by a continent and fifty years, were identical. Grey, just like Queenie, was "a grey dog wearing a sable tunic . . . all her ribs were visible." Both were frequently mistaken for wolves. Queenie only bit Ackerley once, mistaking his hand for an apple. Grey never bit me, but she did take a nip. I was on the telephone, pacing around the apartment in a dressing gown—it was one of the first mornings I had woken there alone. Grey, herding me, nudged her way in and nipped my penis. It was a chilling moment: a playful warning, grotesquely symbolic, to keep in line. I remember it like an electric shock.

My Dog Tulip is considered one of the great dog books: it is much more. Ackerley's intent was to "restore the beastliness to the lives of beasts," and in this he was undoubtedly successful—when Tulip catches a rabbit, the writer hears "the crunch of the tender bones and the skull, bone still warm with the lust of the young creature's life." But the choice of the word "beastliness," a nineteenth-century euphemism for same-sex desire, is crucial. Homosexuality was not to become legal in Great Britain until 1967, the year Ackerley died; his other great work, *My Father and Myself,* in which he took candor about his sexuality to new heights, was not published until after his death.

With Christopher Isherwood calling *My Dog Tulip* "one of the greatest masterpieces of animal literature," one might wonder whether the whole thing is simply an arch exercise in double entendre. Certainly there are passages that read that way: when Ackerley chances to meet Chick, a rough-set owner of male Alsatians, he wants their dogs to mate immediately: "There aren't really many people about . . . can't we go over into those bushes? No-one would see us there." ("Dogging" is the modern word.) Then there's Mr. Plum: "I invited him up for a glass of sherry; but although he was clearly tempted, he thought, after studying his watch, that he had better not, it might make him late for his Sunday dinner, and, well, you know, when one was married that didn't do . . . I did not press him."

My Dog Tulip is therefore about both beasts and beastliness, but it is how Ackerley manages to tread this perfect, shocking line that brings the book close to perfection. Frederic Warburg, Ackerley's publisher, wisely sent the manuscript to a lawyer, enquiring whether it might "deprave or corrupt those dogs into whose paws it might fall."

Within the first two pages, Ackerley has us digging among exposed sinews, internal tumors, and opened stomachs—a red flag for the squeamish, the prudish, or those who hide behind euphemism. A few pages later, a forlorn spaniel, symbol of docile domesticity, stands meekly with "a thermometer up its bottom" at the vet's, and Ackerley is discussing his theory of anal secretions ("a subject that has never been aired before," he told Warburg, "so you have a scoop," although whether this was a pun in 1956 I do not know). By the end of chapter two ("Liquids and Solids"), Ackerley himself has become canine, though he feels a "proper dog" only when Tulip "added my urine, which I had been obliged to void, to the other privileged objects of her attention," a sensationally beautiful sentence that describes his dog peeing on his pee.

If Queenie were human, Ackerley could not possibly have described "that small dark bud, her vulva, [becoming] gradually swollen," "the pretty pink of its lining," and her "little button nipples." There is no bad language, though Ackerley does curse twice at a passing bicyclist who nearly hits Tulip as she does her business. Appropriately, for even the swearing is exquisitely handled, he hurls the two epithets "turd" and "arsehole." Ackerley has created a linguistic world where he can call a spade a spade, and trace the causal relationship between an arsehole and a turd, with impunity.

His experience of Tulip's only pregnancy, finally achieved after two chapters of excruciating comedy and some hair-raising straight talking, is too much for Ackerley. He decides that it cannot happen again, though he does not get her spayed. This leads to the dark heart of the book, the climactic fifth chapter, "The Turn of the Screw." Ackerley walks Tulip on Wimbledon Common. Her heat, which he will not allow to be satisfied, disgusts him ("I cannot bear it, she cannot avoid it, she obtrudes it constantly upon my sight") yet he wonders whether she is any worse off than those humans "who seek gratification of it, without respite, over the greater part of our lives" and cunningly contrasts the male dog who is "equipped for it, but the equipment is not used. There is a human conspiracy against him."

Acklerley cannot bear to be in collusion with the agents of repression and debates his decision with his conscience. Man and dog enter a nightmare of broken glass, a bottle's "splintered sides stand up like spears" that will pierce Tulip's pads, her "sponges of blood" that will "open like grapes." St. Sebastian evoked, Ackerley sees a holly thicket and remembers: "last year a man entered it to die." He is referring to an article from the *Times,* June 30, 1926. He then speaks directly to the suicide, Young Holland with his "traits of effeminacy," wondering where precisely he took his life: "Everyone wished you different from what you were, so you came here at last and pushed your face into a swamp, and that was the end of you, perfect but imperfect boy . . . "

As I leafed through the beautiful, surprisingly massive manuscript in the Library, the pages fell open to a photograph of Tulip rolling on her back, looking shockingly like our dead Grey. “Upside down she is white,” read Ackerley’s caption. This is presumably one of the snapshots of Tulip “micturating, crapping and conversing with other dogs” that he submitted to the publishers, assuming they wouldn’t have any use for them. They didn’t.

The finished book is slim, less than 50,000 words. The handwritten manuscript is in excess of 150,000. The edits seem to be almost entirely autobiographical: “I know I am insufferable”; “I am, categorically, a human being, and I am ashamed of being a human being”; “I am 70 years old. I have just been given a delicious dinner by old friends who think I deserve a pat on the back”—wherever he went, he wanted to be treated like a dog—“. . . one cannot disdain friendship. Yet I never wished to be feted and would not have allowed it if I could.” None of these many sad reflections survive in the finished text. They speak of the loneliness of an elderly man whose “ideal partner” is his dog: “Tomorrow is [her] birthday. She will be twelve. Throughout this time she has given me the whole of her heart and demanded the whole of mine. If she could answer questions and was asked if she thought she had received it, she would say yes.”

Truman Capote called *My Dog Tulip* “one of the greatest books ever written by anybody in the world.” It must certainly be the best book that is both entirely about dogs and not about dogs at all, but about love and desire, and the terrible cost of their denial. Queenie gave Ackerley not only a reason to live, to love, and to write, but an opportunity to voice feelings and air issues, the suppression of which drove many to the darkest of places and the depths of despair.

Queenie was a jealous, almost unmanageable dog. *My Dog Tulip,* which seems initially so tame (a Book-of-the-Month Club selection!), is literature at its most unmuzzled.

VICTORIA STEELE, Brooke Russell Astor Director of Collections Strategy

VICTORIA STEELE

The WunderCabinet,
Barbara Hodgson and Claudia Cohen,
Heavenly Monkey Editions, 2011
Spencer Collection

any contributors to this book have chosen older works, some of which have been in the Library's collection for decades. I have chosen an item that, as of this writing, has been in the collection for two weeks. I have selected this work not only because of its intrinsic appeal, but also because it shows that NYPL continues to develop its holdings and to build upon the acquisitions of smart and discerning colleagues, past and present.

Barbara Hodgson and Claudia Cohen, the creators of *The WunderCabinet,* take their inspiration from a long line of collectors, from the Renaissance onward, who have created cabinets of curiosities, or *Wunderkammern,* to display the beautiful, odd, and intriguing objects they have accumulated. Such cabinets have ranged in size from small cupboards of modestly circumstanced connoisseurs to immense rooms of powerful monarchs. Historically speaking, these privately owned collections were the precursors of the museums and galleries of today.

Hodgson and Cohen's "cabinet" is a gorgeous multi-compartmented box covered with wood veneers cut into geometrical *trompe-l'œil* patterns reminiscent of the cupboards of the past. The largest compartment houses an elegantly bound volume, featuring etchings, drawings, and collages. Various small compartments contain an assortment of objects culled from the creators' own collections, such as shells, fossils, plants, optical devices, quartz crystals, silkworm cocoons, plaster casts of molars, doll arms, glass eyeballs, and armillary spheres. One can think of the work as a refined, charming, and delightful mash-up of Ulisse Aldrovandi and Joseph Cornell.

At once serious and playful, *The WunderCabinet* contains an enchantment on every page.

TOM STOPPARD, playwright

TOM STOPPARD

A Serious Comedy for Trivial People (The Importance of Being Earnest), Oscar Wilde

1894

I already knew the handwriting. The first time I had money, I bought an Oscar Wilde letter at auction. I framed it, and I can see it from where I'm sitting. It's a perfect Wildean object, a witty one-sentence rebuff written on one side of a sheet of notepaper from the Albemarle Hotel, Piccadilly, in January 1895, the month before *The Importance of Being Earnest* opened at the St. James's Theatre: "Sir—I have read your letter and I see that to the brazen everything is brass. Your obedient servant Oscar Wilde."

And now here was that familiar hand again, a flowing and rather beautiful hand, always legible despite an unprissy, dashed-off look to it; and here in a very ordinary notebook in a book-lined business-like office in the heart of the building was the first draft of the most perfect modern comedy in the English language. The subtitle, "A Trivial Comedy for Serious People," has been altered by Wilde with the adjectives transposed, but the alteration never made it into the first printed edition.

But the thing that is exciting about the Library's handwritten and typewritten early versions of *The Importance of Being Earnest* is not that they are the imprimatur for the text as we know it. On the contrary, what makes the heart beat faster is that here we have the play from which the actor-manager George Alexander carved out Wilde's masterpiece.

It is Wilde's masterpiece, not Alexander's. Let's be clear about that. But for a working playwright, the fascination and value of these relics is that they are testimony to the collaborative and pragmatic nature of theater. Very often, and perhaps invariably to some degree, the text of a play turns out to be partly a transcription of the event. Between the writing and the performance a great deal can happen.

A great deal did happen to *Earnest.* The most drastic occurred not long before the performance, when Alexander compressed the original four acts into three, depriving us, among much else, of one of the characters, a solicitor who arrives in act two to arrest Ernest in pursuit of an unpaid bill at the Savoy Hotel. Honesty compels me to side with Alexander: the text was indeed long and discursive. But what a thrill it is to turn its pages 116 years after George Alexander (who knew his audience) wielded his blue pencil. Wilde was reported to have told him, "The scene that you feel is superfluous cost me terrible exhausting labour . . . it must have taken fully five minutes to write."

ELIZABETH STREB, choreographer and director of the STREB Lab for Action Mechanics

ELIZABETH STREB

TROUVELOT'S MAGNIFICENT ASTRONOMICAL DRAWINGS/ GOETHE'S *SCIENCE OF COLORS*

Johann Elert Bode,
Joannis Elerti Bode Uranographia
Berlin: for the author. 1801

Johann Wolfgang von Goethe,
Zur Farbenlehre von Goethe
Tubingen: J.G. Cotta. 1810

I chose the phenomenal flying dragon on whose page was a series of scattered and exquisite mechanical drawings . . . and radical, very thinly marked longitude and latitudinal lines that demonstrate early comprehension of the trajectories of the largely undiscovered heavens.

This wild lion/dragon/flying beast took to the air, to outer space as one with so much weight ordinarily would not . . . yet this odd, unfamiliar animal ruled the heavens. It aligns beautifully with my lifelong venture that holds the belief that certainly humans can fly. Flying for humans is impractical, foolish really, surely a full-weighted bone-dense, large-muscled body has no access to the sky . . . and yet a miracle of belief occurs when these bodies float and soar and swoop and eventually crash to earth. However, this creature will never fall, he will never land, never touch down, his provenance is in the high skies, where gravity is too light to matter.

I chose this fascinating book on Goethe's hypothesis of the perception of colors. Without early suppositions, no knowledge is ever gained. As Richard Feynman said: the models are almost always incorrect; however, he mentioned the debates that are catalyzed by them create the future facts. Goethe's color plates were exquisite, yet wrong. This early theory was a mammoth distance from Josef Albers's *Interaction of Color* that was taught to a legion of artists at Yale for decades—as he headed up the Department of Design there. I leafed through this 1810 book containing images of faded color plates in geometric patterns. I felt that I absorbed the permission anew to stab in the dark at my particular questions about motion, notions that many years from now, could well be wrong.

COLM TÓIBÍN, novelist

COLM TÓIBÍN

Cathleen ni Houlihan, William Butler Yeats
manuscript draft in the hand of Lady Gregory,
signed in her hand, undated

Between 1896, when he met Lady Gregory in the house of her neighbor Edward Martyn, and his marriage twenty years later, the poet W.B. Yeats spent the summers at Coole Park, Lady Gregory's house in County Galway in the west of Ireland, using the library and the master bedroom. In the summer of 1901 he had a dream, while staying at Coole. He told Lady Gregory about his dream which was "almost as distinct as a vision, of a cottage where there was well-being and firelight and talk of a marriage, and into the midst of that cottage there came an old woman in a long cloak" who was "Ireland herself, that Cathleen ni Houlihan for whom so many songs have been sung, and about whom so many stories have been told and for whose sake so many have gone to their death."

Yeats and Lady Gregory set to work; the publicity for the play *Cathleen ni Houlihan,* which was performed in Dublin in 1902, with Maud Gonne playing the part of Cathleen, had Yeats as the sole author. It is now clear, however, that while the idea belonged to him and he wrote the chant of the old woman at the end, most of the play was, in fact, written by Lady Gregory. Yeats's mind created metaphors and symbols; he could not write ordinary peasant dialogue, or set domestic scenes. The power of the ending, when the old woman is transformed and has "the walk of a Queen," depends on the naturalistic setting that comes before—the talk of money and marriage, the sense of ease in family life in a smallholding in the west of Ireland.

In the manuscript of the play, held in the Berg Collection at The New York Public Library, Lady Gregory has written in pencil on the first section of ten pages, "All this mine alone," and "This with WBY" at the beginning of the second section. Although Yeats gave Lady Gregory credit for other work on which they collaborated, he did not give her much credit for *Cathleen ni Houlihan.* In a diary entry in 1925, Lady Gregory complained that his failure to acknowledge her was "rather hard on me." When her family urged her to insist in public that she was co-author, she said that she could not take from Yeats "any part of what had proved, after all, his one real popular success."

The play packed the hall every night and had an enormous influence on the young revolutionaries in Dublin. In the theater world, it was known that most of its lines had not been written by Yeats, and that it was indeed, for the most part, Lady Gregory's alone. Both the writer Lennox Robinson and the actor Willie Fay, for example, let others know this. When Yeats proudly introduced himself at the time of the riots in the Abbey Theatre in 1907 against *The Playboy of the Western World* as "the author of *Cathleen ni Houlihan,*"the diarist Joseph Holloway noted: "The odd thing is that Fay told me that Lady Gregory wrote the whole of it except the part of *Cathleen.*"

CALVIN TRILLIN, journalist, food writer, humorist, poet, memoirist, and novelist

CALVIN TRILLIN

Various Items on the Subject of Nauru

In 1968, I visited the Republic of Nauru, a remote, eight-square-mile Pacific island made mostly of phosphate. At the time, many Nauruans were becoming prosperous from phosphate royalties while their country was being hauled away in large ships. (Phosphate mining leaves nothing but gnarled coral pinnacles.) Other than contract phosphate-workers, few outsiders visited Nauru—the only way to get there by plane was on a flight that operated from Fiji once every two weeks—and apparently no outsider could speak the Nauruan language. (To me, the Nauruan word for *motorcycle* sounded like a motorcycle, and all other Nauruan words sounded like the Nauruan word for *motorcycle*.)

Twenty years later, when I was preparing for a return trip to Nauru, I went to The New York Public Library to read some back issues of a monthly that covered Pacific islands. While I was there, it occurred to me to look in the card catalog. I didn't expect to find much of anything; after all, hardly anybody in America had ever heard of Nauru. What I found astonished me. There were dozens of items. The Library had the constitution of Nauru. It had a report to the Council of the League of Nations on the administration of Nauru while it was being administered as a trust territory between world wars. It had a monograph on the string figures of Nauru. It had books on Nauru in German and French and a couple of languages I didn't recognize. A user of The New York Public Library could have written a book on Nauru without leaving 42nd Street.

Since then, when I think of the wonders of the Library's collections, what comes to mind is not some priceless treasure—the Gutenberg Bible, say, or one of the fourteen original copies of the Bill of Rights. What comes to mind is the Republic of Nauru.

THE TUCK FAMILY (l to r): Lauran, Jayson, and Justin Tuck, defensive end for The New York Giants

THE TUCK FAMILY

Mother Goose or The Old Nursery Rhymes
Illustrated by Kate Greenaway
1882

NEIL DEGRASSE TYSON, astrophysicist and director of Hayden Planetarium, American Museum of Natural History

NEIL DEGRASSE TYSON

Sidereus nuncius, Galileo Galilei
1653

Philosophiæ naturalis principia mathematica
Sir Isaac Newton
1687

De revolvtionibvs, Nicolaus Copernicus
1543

I know that I am mortal by nature and ephemeral, but when I trace at my pleasure the windings to and fro of the heavenly bodies, I no longer touch earth with my feet. I stand in the presence of Zeus himself and take my fill of ambrosia.
—*Ptolemy*

I was nine when I knew I wanted to be become an astrophysicist. It happened during my first visit to the American Museum of Natural History's Hayden Planetarium, where I now work. I grew up in the Bronx, where there is no sky. I visited the planetarium when I was just old enough to be struck by it, leaving me convinced that I didn't choose the universe; the universe came down and chose me that day in the planetarium under the stars.

As a scientist, and in particular as an astrophysicist, I have a special caring and respect for people who came before me—all those who struggled to understand the operations of the world. I think anyone who looks up at night and wonders where we come from and where we are going—not only scientists—senses the magnitude of the universe and the wonder it still holds for us.

These three books represent fundamental shifts in our understanding of our place in the universe. Copernicus looked at the night sky and tried to understand the movements of the planets. In doing so, he overturned a concept that had been rampant for one and a half millennia. He was the first since the philosophers of ancient Greece to see Earth as a moving part of the universe rather than its static center. He challenged all notions about our place in the natural world.

Not until sixty years later would Galileo generate the first telescopic data to support Copernicus's heliocentric theories. Galileo reveals to us that the universe is knowable and the human mind has access to it just by the power of experiment combined with the power of thought. Another sixty years later, Newton would come along with equations that predict the behavior of objects. Newton revealed to us that the universe is comprehensible—that we have the power of prediction. One of the most important features of a scientific theory is your ability to predict the outcome.

When I look back on these works, I imagine reading them for the first time, when they were first published. In this way I commune through time, as I reflect on our intellectual and philosophical relationship to the natural world.

VAMPIRE WEEKEND (Ezra Koenig, Rostam Batmanglij, Chris Tomson, and Chris Baio), musicians

VAMPIRE WEEKEND

Four[4], John Cage

John Cage Music Mansuscript Collection, 1991

HAROLD VARMUS, scientist and director of the National Cancer Institute

HAROLD VARMUS

David Copperfield, Charles Dickens
A Reading. In Five Chapters.

London: Privately printed [by W. Clowes, 1866]
author's copy, with his manuscript notes and corrections

Exactly fifty years ago, while working on my senior thesis at Amherst College, I devoted a large part of each day to reading and thinking about Charles Dickens, both his life and his novels. Yet—except for some quick glimpses of his handwritten manuscripts in dusty cabinets of the British Museum during a post-graduation European walkabout—I had not looked closely at or held in my hand any pages on which Dickens personally labored, until NYPL opened its repository to me on December 4, 2010.

In the nearly fifty-year interval between my thesis and my visit to NYPL, I have drifted quite far from my earlier intentions to become a scholar and teacher of English literature. Aside from occasional re-readings of *Great Expectations* and quick re-openings of many volumes of his novels when moving house, I have spent very few hours in Dickens's company since my thesis was submitted. However, the pages that I chose for inspection in December—hand-edited passages of his work that Dickens excerpted to stage his famous public readings, including those in New York and other American destinations—connected with what remains of my thesis-writing, Dickens-obsessed student persona.

In my thesis, I had stressed the relationship between Dickens's narrative voice in complex novels that pit good against evil and his reigning presence in a sometimes tumultuous private life. In the novels, admirable but weak characters were often saved by violent, often murderous, narrative solutions to threats against them by ingenious and intriguing villains. In his private life, Dickens lavished protective love on those he considered pure and powerless, like the ailing sister-in-law with whom he was famously infatuated. These dramatic tensions were sometimes displayed in his frequent public readings and were partly responsible for their appeal.

Readings by novelists like Dickens, who usually published their work unabridged in periodicals, one segment at a time, were enormously popular forms of public entertainment in England and America in the nineteenth century and quite unlike today's readings during publicity tours. For most of Dickens's audiences, the novels were often first heard, rather than read, when friends and neighbors gathered to hear the latest episode in a compelling story—for instance, when new issues of journals like *Household Words* arrived on our shores. To have the author himself do the reading must have been a remarkably exciting event, and many accounts confirm that both of Dickens's long reading tours in the United States—in 1842 and in 1867–68—were very well received, especially in the East Coast cities. (New Yorkers were well known to be avid followers of his novels. When the ship bearing the installment of *The Old Curiosity Shop* likely to reveal the outcome of little Nell's illness was nearing New York Harbor, those on board could hear a devoted chorus of Dickens's fans on the shore calling out, "Is little Nell dead?")

But more was involved in the appreciation of those readings than just an audience's excitement about seeing the famous author. Dickens himself was passionate about the readings as acts of theatrical fulfillment. Dickens had his own aspirations to work in the theater, played in amateur productions, and met his later-life companion, the well-known actress Ellen Ternan, when they were part of a cast. (The liaison ultimately led to the breakup of Dickens's marriage.)

To prepare for his public readings, Dickens practiced extensively and enthusiastically in private. I recall reading fifty years ago a frightening account by a visitor to Dickens's home in Kent, Gad's Hill, who feared that some terrible event was occurring behind the house as he walked up the path. It turned out that Dickens was in his yard practicing his reading of an especially violent scene from *Oliver Twist,* adding vigorous motions and cries to the text.

So I assumed that when NYPL allowed me to see his "scripts" for the American readings of 1867–68 I would find typescripts with emphatic markings—underlinings and exclamation points and indications for dramatic pauses. Instead, what I was given was much more programmed and analytic. The small volume of selected excerpts from *David Copperfield* had been printed by W. Clowes in 1866, in only a very few copies, expressly for Dickens's use during the readings. The pages were carefully, even meticulously, edited in Dickens's hand, with many changes of single words and punctuation, some large deletions of text, occasional entries of new sentences, and insertions of new words to smooth transitions, especially across deleted regions. The flavor of the editing and the handwriting evoked careful professionalism, not the theatrical emotionalism reported by the visitor to Gad's Hill—and by some observers following performances.

Given my sensibility as a college student writing a thesis on Dickens entitled "The Murder of Evil," it is perhaps not surprising that the impression I retained of Dickens' readings was focused on their theatricality and high emotion. But as the slim volume placed before me in December reminded me, Dickens doubtless also played to many audiences interested in hearing some of his most famous, sentimental, and non-violent passages—from *The Old Curiosity Shop, A Christmas Carol* (especially), and (of course) *David Copperfield.* It was apparent from the annotated pages that he was careful to guarantee clarity and readability, attributes that would secure the affection of his long-term fans while providing an evening of gentle entertainment.

I am pleased that The New York Public Library has the resources required to safeguard this small link between Charles Dickens and the literary habits of New Yorkers, and I am grateful that its staff were willing to show the slim, precious volume to me on a Saturday afternoon.

MADELEINE VILJOEN, curator of prints, The Miriam and Ira D. Wallach Division of Art, Prints and Photographs

MADELEINE VILJOEN

The Annunciation, Federico Barocci

etching with engraving and drypoint, 1584,
Print Collection, Miriam and Ira D. Wallach
Division of Art, Prints and Photographs

Federico Barocci, the author of *The Annunciation,* was a Capuchin monk and one of the most important Italian painters of the late sixteenth century. When the printmaker he had hired to produce engravings after his paintings died prematurely, Barocci set out to teach himself to create his own prints using the medium of etching. Between 1581 and 1584, he made just four prints. While the first of these is quite amateurish, by the time he created *The Annunciation,* the artist had acquired a staggering facility with the etching needle. The work reproduces his 1584 painting commissioned by the Duke of Urbino for Loreto, now in the Vatican Museum. Passages of the work thrill, including the dense black lines of crosshatching that shroud and envelop the figures, the stipple dots that describe the Virgin's smooth cheek or the sleek contours of a sleeping cat, and finally the artist's signature that accommodates itself illusionistically to the image's steeply sloped ground plane.

As recently as the twentieth century, the Calcografia in Rome pulled close to two hundred impressions of the etching, attesting to the work's long-lasting appeal. The figures in those works had been reworked with a burin, however, and the matrix plated with chromium, resulting in works that are dull and lifeless in comparison with The New York Public Library's print, which scholars acknowledge as one of the artist's finest lifetime impressions.

SARAH VOWELL, author, journalist, essayist, and social commentator

(previous pages)
SARAH VOWELL studying a map
of the Oregon Trail Congress

SARAH VOWELL

CHARLES PREUSS

Charles Preuss, Map of the Oregon Trail Congress
1846

hen we think of the Frémont expeditions to map the American West in the 1840s, as we so often do, we think of the expedition's scout, the famous fur trapper and mountaineer Kit Carson. Or we mull over John Charles Frémont himself, the spirited, flashing light of a man from whom Las Vegas's flashy lit-up Fremont Street would one day get its name.

In 1842, the United States government sent Frémont to lead one of the most important expeditions of the nineteenth century, to what would come to be called the Oregon Trail. To make maps and drawings along the way, Frémont employed a German immigrant named Charles Preuss. Frémont's lively report to Congress on his findings, illustrated with Preuss's drawings and maps, became a bestseller. And Preuss's map of the Oregon Trail Congress, published in 1846, was soon crammed into the glove box of every Conestoga rolling west.

If you ever had to reach across a copy of the *Book of Mormon* blocking the parmesan cheese at a pizza place outside of Provo, it is because Brigham Young was so intrigued with Frémont's description of the area surrounding Utah's Great Salt Lake he promptly moved his Mormon brethren there.

So Charles Preuss was one of the most important, influential, and talented cartographers of his generation. Problem was, this excellent mapmaker just so happened to loathe pretty much every minute of actual exploring.

Preuss's diaries from his three trips out west with Frémont seethe with manly gung-ho, cowboy bravery like, "I wish I were at the market with a shopping basket."

Mulling over the roasting mule meat that is to be his dinner, Preuss sighed, "What a treat it would be with a bottle of wine—but stop, that thought is too beautiful."

John Charles Frémont was Manifest Destiny's advance man. As a young surveyor he had cut his teeth mapping the Cherokee lands in the Southeast in the 1830s so the U.S. government had an accurate account of the real estate it was about to steal. Later on, Frémont came home from his expeditions out west a hero and celebrity. His nickname? "The Pathfinder." He went on to become the first presidential candidate of the Republican Party. And the signature image trotted out for his later self-promotion, including his presidential campaign, was one incident from his western journeys. It became the iconic moment of his life, what crossing the Delaware was for Washington, what tripping over the ottoman was for Dick Van Dyke. Frémont climbed alone to what he thought was the highest peak in the Rockies, stood up straight and tall, and jabbed an American flag into the mountaintop, Old Glory whipping defiantly in the icy wind.

Think about the kind of person you have to be to do that, to be so unapologetically grand. Preuss, meanwhile, was farther down the mountain, striking a less Neil Armstrong-y pose:

> *I slipped, sat down on my pants, and slid downhill at a great speed. Although I made all efforts to hold back by trying to dig my fingers into the icy crust. I slid down about two hundred feet, until the bare rocks stopped me again . . . When I arrived, I rolled over twice and got away with two light bruises, one on my right arm and one on my arse. The pain made me sit still for a few minutes.*

Frémont wrote of this climb that "standing where never human foot had stood before" he "felt the exaltation of first explorers."

Preuss put it this way: "All of my pants are torn."

Was Preuss at least delighted by the expedition's opportunity for fresh air? To him, the ever present sagebrush and tumbleweeds made the West smell like a pharmacy. Did he find some solace in the stunning views of the Colorado Rockies? It reminded him of a trip to the Swiss Alps he took when he was a young man. He writes, "Now, if I compare that view with the one I see today, it is as though I were to turn my eyes from the face of a lovely girl to the wrinkled face of an old woman."

Reading an entry from Preuss's diary from July 1843, I came across a sentence beginning with the words "I enjoyed." I was so relieved for Preuss. Yay! He got to enjoy something. But the sentence keeps going, "I enjoyed nothing but mosquitoes."

Preuss's resentment of the bugs, the landscape, the Indians, and the monotony pales compared to his many, varied flip-outs about food. His entry for June 12, 1842, cheers up with the slaughter of an ox. Preuss thinks that after the meat ages overnight, "Tomorrow, to be sure, it will taste excellent." The next entry on June 13 reports, "It did not taste excellent."

Preuss has an entire subset of food complaints involving salt and the lack thereof. When they run out of salt near the Great Salt Lake he cracks, "Isn't that funny?" One of his happiest entries takes place in the Sierra mountains on February 15, 1844, near what is now the California–Nevada border. He reports, "The great good news is that the men have bartered rock salt from the Indians. Just now Taplin is bringing in a big lump." Preuss was so giddy about the salt that he doesn't mention what the expedition was doing while they were waiting around for the seasoning to show up: discovering Lake Tahoe.

It makes sense that Preuss, a man who was outstanding at measuring and drawing and using barometric data to construct a two-dimensional, topographical representation of a mountain might suck at climbing said mountain. Cartography was Preuss's calling, but in order for him to do the job he loved to do, he had to live a life he hated.

The thing I admire most about Charles Preuss is that Frémont, his boss, apparently had no idea just how miserable the cartographer was on the job. Preuss's diaries were meant for one reader, his wife, and they weren't published until 1958, after Preuss and all his colleagues had been dead for a century. In fact, Frémont commended Preuss for "his even temper and patient endurance of hardship," noting Preuss had a "cheerful philosophy of his own, which often brightened dark situations."

Cheerful philosophy such as, "No clouds to be seen, no rain in sight, and no trees to be found. The warm wind blows sand and dust into our eyes. Our last three oxen refused to go farther and were put to death."

Charles Preuss hung himself outside of Washington in 1854. Once, out West, he confided in his journal, "The question of whether we shall have bread and coffee tonight or no bread and coffee is a much more important question than to be or not to be."

The other people on these expeditions, John Charles Frémont and his legendary scout, Kit Carson, are the sort of grand, hearty, how-the-West-was-won figures who are easily made into colossal statues. But there's something comforting, even heroic, about a human-scale footnote like Preuss, a man who made history even though all he ever wanted was to make maps.

WABC-TV NEWS ANCHORS (l to r): Diana Williams, Sade Baderinwa, Bill Ritter, Liz Cho, Lori Stokes, Ken Rosato

WABC-TV NEWS ANCHORS

photographed in the DeWitt Wallace Periodical Room

JAY WALDER, chairman and CEO of the Metropolitan Transportation Authority

JAY WALDER

Honus Wagner Baseball Card

Leopold Morse Goulston Baseball Collection
1909

That a rare Honus Wagner baseball card could be found at The New York Public Library was a fantastic surprise for me. I discovered during a decade-long stay in London that baseball is a sport that can be enjoyed almost as much by its traditions as by watching it being played. Taking the kids to the ballpark wasn't an option for us. So we relied on other things. Reading the box scores the day after a game allowed us to visually re-create it in our minds. And bringing back a few packs of baseball cards would be my treat after a trip back home. We could sit together putting the cards in three-ring binders and challenge each other with the stats on the back. Wagner's stats remain impressive. He led the league in batting eight times, stolen bases five times, and his play in 1908 is sometimes cited as the greatest single season for any player in baseball history. His card is rare and valuable, not just because it is old, but because Wagner withdrew permission to have his card reproduced, deciding that he did not want to be associated with tobacco—the original promotional vehicle for baseball card distribution. Admirable, and ahead of his time. His time—the days when he was piling up stats for the record books—was the early twentieth century, the years when the Library and the New York City Subway were being built. It was a very good time for New York.

Help The New York Public Library thrive for another 100 years!

If you use the Library, or if you simply appreciate this great democratic center of learning and discovery, you can play an important role in its mission by becoming a Friend to The New York Public Library.

Thanks to the generous support of Friends, the Library continues to provide books and information, as well as research and educational programs, to the millions of users who visit us in person or online. Your contribution will help us sustain essential Library services valued by people in New York, across the country, and around the world.

Visit nypl.org/support to join us today.

PENGUIN CLASSICS
AESCHYLUS
The Oresteia
Agamemnon, The Libation Bearers, The Eumenides
Translated by ROBERT FAGLES

PENGUIN CLASSICS
JOHN STEINBECK
The Grapes of Wrath

MAN
MUST
LIVE
PENGUIN CLASSICS
ES'KIA MPHAHLELE
In Corner B

PENGUIN CLASSICS
JACK KEROUAC
On the Road

PENGUIN CLASSICS DELUXE EDITIONS

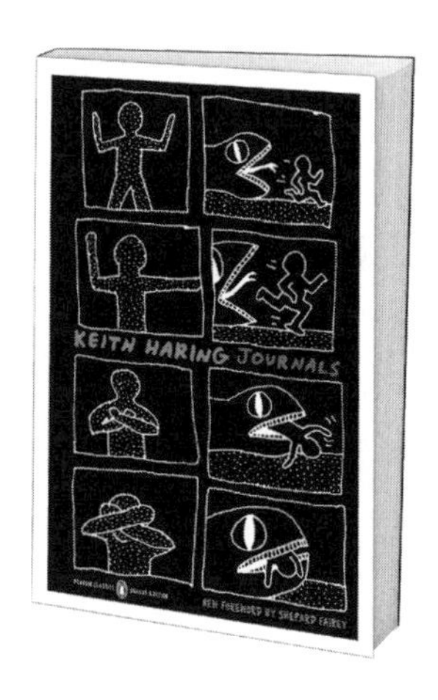

Penguin Classics has generously underwritten the publication of *Know the Past, Find the Future.* Additional support for the Library's Centennial Festival has been made possible through an endowment established by family and friends of the late Richard B. Salomon, and by Bank of America, The Skeel Fund, MetLife Foundation, The Blackstone Charitable Foundation, Asprey, Wells Fargo, *The Wall Street Journal,* the Metropolitan Transportation Authority, Titan, WABC-TV, Penguin Classics, and *Gotham Magazine.*

Know the Past, Find the Future:
Project Director: Dennis Swaim, Penguin Books
Designer: Lynn Rogan, Penguin Books
Page Layout: Jessica Reed, Penguin Books

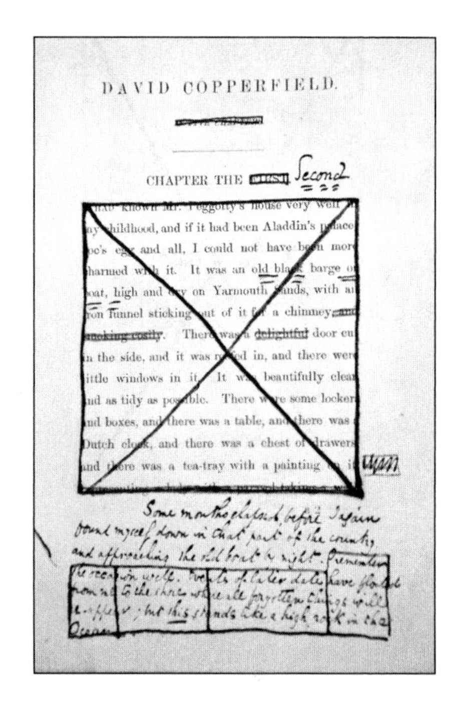
DAVID COPPERFIELD.

CHAPTER THE Second

childhood, and if it had been Aladdin's
and all, I could not have mor
harmed it. It was an old barge o
oat, high and on Yarmouth ands, with a
ron funnel sticking ut of it a chimney
. There door cu
n the side, and it was in, and there wer
ittle windows in it. It beautifully clea
nd as tidy as po There some locker
nd boxes, and here was a table, and here was
Dutch clo and there was a chest o drawers
and ere was a tea-tray with a painting

Some months elapsed before I again
found myself down in that part of the country,
and approaching the old boat by night.